Crazy Quilting

Crazy Quilting

Christine Dabbs

Edited by Carter Houck

Rutledge Hill Press®
NASHVILLE, TENNESSEE

To Frances and Jennifer

Published by Rutledge Hill Press®, 211 Seventh Avenue North, Nashville, Tennessee 37219.
Distributed in Canada by H. B. Fenn & Company, Ltd., 34 Nixon Road, Bolton, Ontario L7E 1W2.
Distributed in Australia by The Five Mile Press Pty., Ltd., 22 Summit Road, Noble Park, Victoria 3174.
Distributed in New Zealand by Tandem Press, 2 Rugby Road, Birkenhead, Auckland 10.
Distributed in the United Kingdom by Verulam Publishing, Ltd., 152a Park Street Lane, Park Street, St. Albans, Hertfordshire AL2 2AU.

Where Love Resides is a registered trademark of Universal City Studios, Inc., and Amblin Entertainment, Inc. All rights reserved.

How to Make an American Quilt is a registered trademark and copyright 1995 of Universal City Studios, Inc., and Amblin Entertainment, Inc. All rights reserved.

Quote from the novel How to Make an American Quilt by Whitney Otto printed with permission of Random House, Inc., New York, New York.

Shand Kydd frieze peacock printed with permission of Imperial Home Decor Group, Belgrave Mills, Belgrave Road, Darwen, Lancashire, England.

Design and typesetting by Bateman Design

Library of Congress Cataloging-in-Publication Data

Dabbs, Christine, 1950–
    Crazy quilting / Christine Dabbs : edited by Carter Houck.
      p. cm.
    Includes bibliographical references.
    ISBN 1-55853-694-9 (pb)
      1. Patchwork—Patterns. 2. Crazy quilts—United States.
    I. Houck, Carter.   II. Title.
    TT835.D32   1998   98–41975
    746.46'041—dc21   CIP

Printed in the Republic of China.

1 2 3 4 5 6 7 8 9 — 03 02 01 00 99 98

Contents

Acknowledgments

I WOULD LIKE TO EXPRESS my sincere appreciation and gratitude to Cordie Gary, Kelly Gallagher-Abbott, and Barbara Brown for their never-ending support of my crazy-quilt endeavors; Greg and Barri Brown, Darlene Hoadley, and Eleanor Miller for sharing their crazy quilts; Arthur Rose and Andrew Dhuey for their legal assistance; Beverly and Robert Walker of Cameo House Fine Photography for their efforts in photographing the quilts; Carter Houck for her advice, knowledge, and guidance; and my husband, Christopher, for his help and computer skills when I needed them.

Introduction

MY INTRODUCTION to crazy quilts began one afternoon in 1986 when my mother showed me a crazy-quilt top that had been in my family since 1892. She had tucked it away in the closet for safekeeping when I was a young girl, where it had remained ever since. I had always loved needlework and found myself fascinated by the various fabrics, embroidered motifs, and decorative stitching on the quilt top. I studied it for hours, making notes and drawing stitches, thinking that someday I'd love to stitch a crazy quilt for my daughters, Frances and Jennifer. The quilt was never far from my mind, and several years later I decided that it was time to take up the challenge and stitch a crazy quilt.

When I embarked on this new adventure, I went to my local quilt shop to search for information on crazy quilts and how to make one. The books I found offered historical information and small projects but lacked directions that would enable me to create an entire quilt. Thus, I decided that the best teacher would be old crazy quilts themselves. Each quilt I studied illuminated the love and great care the quiltmaker put into its creation, regardless of how simple or elaborate the fabrics and decorative stitching were. Many of these quilts are missing provenance, adding an element of mystery to the family history and memories stitched into them.

The popularity of crazy quilts peaked in America during the Victorian Era, 1875 to 1900. Although such quilts were considered by some to be a fad and a rebellion against tradition, they offered women an opportunity to express their artistic talents through needlework. At the 1876 Centennial Exposition in Philadelphia, exhibits from the Royal School of Art Needlework and in the Japanese Pavilion had a significant influence on women, providing inspiration for their crazy quilts. Women created these artistic quilts to beautify their homes and to display their expertise with a needle and thread. Random patches for these quilts were stitched together from a diverse assortment of fabrics, such as silk, satin, velvet, taffeta, and moiré, or from wool, flannel, and cotton. Silk companies were able to take advantage of the popularity of crazy quilts by offering packages of silk remnants for sale through the mail. Some of the silk patches on many of these old quilts have deteriorated over time, while others remain in very good condition. The brittle cracking or shredding of the patches can be attributed to the "weighting" of the silk with mineral salts during the manufacturing process.

Widely circulated women's magazines encouraged and supported the crazy-quilt phenomenon through articles and by printing popular motifs, such as the Kate Greenaway designs, that could be embroidered or painted onto the quilt patches. As a result, quilts from all regions of the country often contain identical motifs. Additionally, many quilts incorporated such personal details as names, initials, dates, places, and in some cases, commemorative ribbons or bits of lace and beads.

Initially, the most desirable crazy quilts were those which were heavily embroidered, but toward the end of the 1890s, their popularity declined as people grew tired of their ostentatiousness. A tendancy toward less extravagant embroidery ensued as crazy quilting began to give way to less structured patterns. Since this decline, crazy quilts generally have been recognized only in the historical content of books or museum exhibits, until the 1980s.

Over the past several decades, the quilting community has grown, and the limits of design, style, and content of traditional and art quilts have expanded. In the 1980s crazy quilts began to experience a resurgence, helped in part by the growing popularity of silk ribbon embroidery and embellishments.

In 1994 I wished to exhibit my crazy quilts but discovered all quilt-show entries must be quilted, i.e., "no tied quilts allowed." This rule would exclude most crazy quilts because, by the nature of their construction, they usually are not quilted but are instead tied or tacked. Early in 1995 I corresponded with the American Quilter's Society, the International Quilt Association, and the National Quilt Association, requesting an exception to their "no tied quilts" rule. The International Quilt Association responded positively by adding a new crazy-quilt category to its annual exhibition, beginning in 1995. With this recognition and crazy quilts' continued growth in popularity, many independent quilt shows have begun to accept crazy-quilt entries. In January 1998 the Quilt Heritage Foundation established The Crazy Quilt Society, which offers support for crazy quilters, a newsletter and an annual conference.

As quiltmaking reaches new levels as an art form, it is my hope that quilters will combine the knowledge from the past with new ideas and inspiration to create their own crazy quilt heirlooms.

THE CRAZY QUILT was a fad of the nineteenth century and as such is not truly considered art, yet still it has its devotees. It is comprised of remnants of material in numerous textures, colors; actually, you could not call the squares of a crazy quilt squares, since the stitched-together pieces are of all sizes and shapes. This is the pattern with the least amount of discipline and the greatest measure of emotion.

— Whitney Otto in *How to Make an American Quilt*

Part 1
The Crazy Quilts

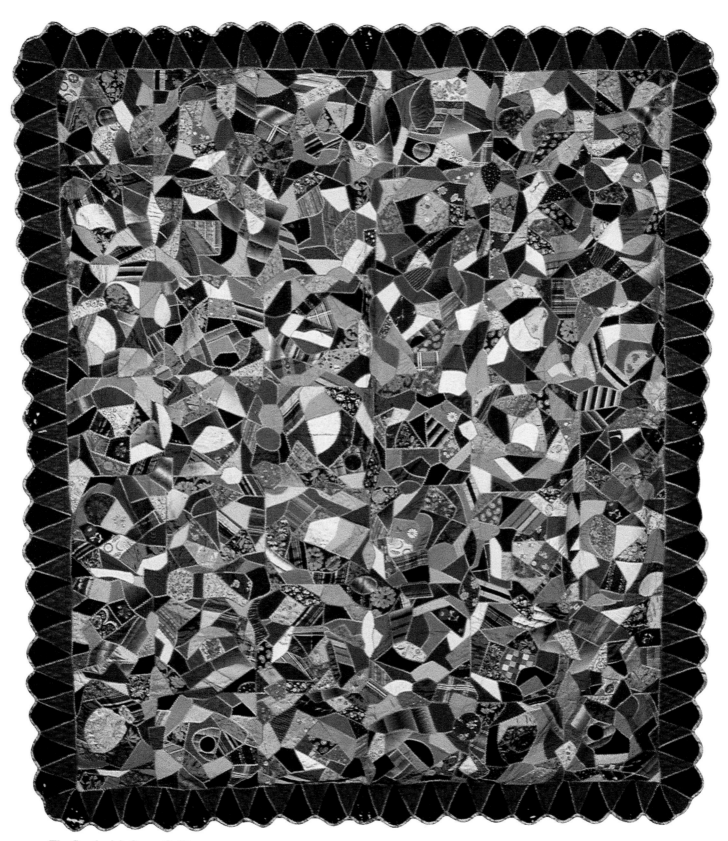

The Southwick Crazy Quilt
Size: *66″ x 78″*
Date: *1898*
Maker: *Elizabeth Southwick*
           born: 1834, England

The Southwick Crazy Quilt

THE SOUTHWICK CRAZY QUILT gives the illusion of being pieced on one large foundation, but it actually is assembled from forty-two individual 10-by-10-inch blocks. The foundation fabric blocks are lightweight brown cotton twill and polished cotton.

The silk fabric samples and scraps that make up the quilt top are stunning. The diverse silk brocade designs include flowers, birds, paisley, Japanese prints, bugs, and butterflies. Six different brocades are represented, each in a variety of color schemes. Several silk fabrics are reversed; thus, front and back sides are used as patches on the quilt top. Surprisingly, only a few pieces of velvet are seen on this quilt. The color schemes are soft blues and greens, muted purple and green, rust, beige, maroon, orange, brown, and navy blue. There are also many ribbons with flower brocades, stripes, and plaids.

The silk patches were first appliquéd to the foundation blocks, which were then hand stitched together. Next, additional silk patches were appliquéd over the block seam lines to create the illusion of a single foundation. There are 1,103 silk patches within the border of this crazy-quilt top.

The Southwick quilt is entirely hand stitched and consists of five layers: 1) the crazy patches, 2) crazy-patch foundation, 3) backing foundation, 4) batting, and 5) backing. Every crazy-patch seam is covered with a small, even, herringbone stitch, using a variegated silk thread in shades ranging from rust to orange to yellow.

The quilt back has three layers and could be a separate quilt itself. Its foundation consists of a plain-weave cotton fabric, lightweight batting, and a soft, green-and-white-striped silk fabric that forms the outer quilt back. These three layers are hand quilted together with brown thread in a grid pattern.

The border, 3 1/2 to 4 inches wide, is constructed from a triangle-and-scallop pattern in alternating black and maroon silk fabric.

The quilted back and crazy-patch top are joined together in the triangle-and-scallop border with additional grid quilting through all five layers. They are attached only in the border, with the center part of the top and back not joined but separate. A 3/8-inch striped-silk binding is hand stitched over the scalloped edge.

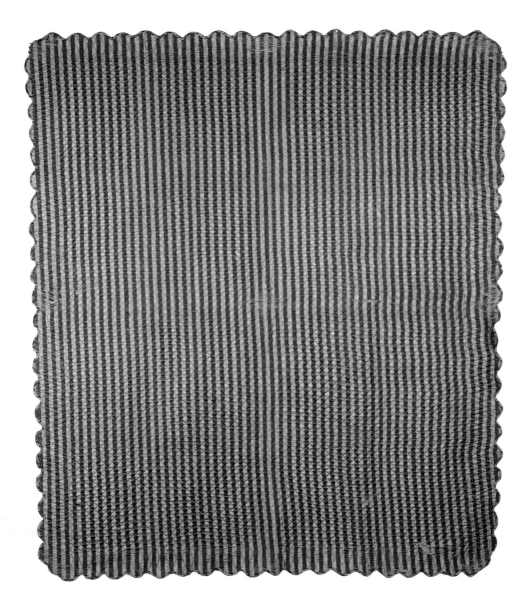

Striped-silk quilted back,
the Southwick Crazy Quilt,
1898, 66″ x 78″.

The Southwick and Colby Families

Eva Southwick and William Colby were married in 1894 and purchased a house on Church Street in Lockport, New York, where they lived for more than thirty years. The couple were proprietors of a grocery store in their working-class neighborhood, which included numerous immigrants from England, Ireland, and Scotland. In the mid-1890s Eva's mother, Elizabeth, became a widow and moved from the family farm in Pennsylvania to live with the Colbys in Lockport. While Eva and William worked in the store, Elizabeth cared for the couple's only child, Marjorie, with the help of May Goffney, a sixteen-year-old servant girl who lived with the family.

Elizabeth became friends with Susan Cunningham, a dressmaker by profession, and the widow Margaret Sawyer, a tailor, who both lived in the boarding house next door. It was from these friends that Elizabeth received many of the silk fabric samples and scraps used in her crazy quilt. Elizabeth lived well into her eighties, and upon her passing, the quilt was given to Marjorie. Elizabeth's crazy quilt was passed on in the family, until it eventually was left for sale at an antique consignment shop, where I purchased it in 1994.

Note the even herringbone stitches covering the seams.

The Snyder Crazy Quilt

Size: 72″ x 72″
Date: 1899
Maker: Mary J. Snyder
            born: December 7, 1852

The Snyder Crazy Quilt

THIS CRAZY QUILT contains sixteen 18-by-18-inch blocks. The fabrics used as the foundation for the individual blocks include cotton twills, wool, and shirting material with flower prints, plaids, stripes, and solid colors. The crazy patches are hand pieced and appliquéd onto the foundation blocks with coarse thread.

The patches are made from men's wool suits in winter colors of gray, black, brown, and beige, with contrasting patches of blue denim, red wool, and a red wool knit sweater. The heavy weight of these fabrics may be related to the coldness of Ohio winters and this crazy quilt's intended use. The blocks are put together with hand stitching.

The embroidery and decorative seam stitching is simple yet elegant. There are two embroidered motifs: a flower repeated on five patches and a flying bird repeated on three. The names, dates, and phrases on the quilt are embroidered in a stem stitch. Six family members are represented: Mary and Isaac Snyder; their sons, Charlie and Willie; a grandmother, Elizabeth Smith; and an aunt, Katie Long. The importance of family, home, love, and friendship is expressed in a few simple embroidered phrases: "Welcome to All," "Welcome Home," "Good Friend," "Love," "To All Our Friends," "Yours Truely," and "Home Sweet Home."

Mary's mother embroidered one of the three birds seen on the quilt. The phrase "Elizabeth Smith made this bird, I am 71 March the 10, 1899" is embroidered across two patches next to this bird. Another embroidered phrase, "Aunt Katie Long is here March 28, 1898," did not fit entirely on one patch and was extended onto an adjacent patch.

The most endearing sentiment is Mary's to her son, which states, "This To Rememberence of Charlies Mother." (Charles had joined the infantry in 1898 and was sent to Cuba.) Also embroidered on patches are "Rememberme and Forgetme Not."

The embroidery, stem stitching, and decorative seam coverings are stitched entirely with thin twine, accented with red yarn. The yarn has begun to wear and disappear in places, but the twine is like new. The predominant stitches used to cover the seams are straight, feather, cretan, and buttonhole variations. The decorative seam stitching is very evenly spaced, and the cotton batting is dense, although not heavy or thick.

The quilt back is made from three machine-stitched panels of what appears to be cotton drapery fabric. The quilt top, batting, and back are secured together with ties of red yarn evenly spaced every 4 inches, and the edges are machine stitched together. Mary made this heavy winter quilt from materials she had available. It has no decorative border, perhaps because she planned to tuck in the quilt when the bed was made.

"This To Rememberence Of Charlies Mother" quilt block; the Snyder Crazy Quilt, 1899, 72″ x 72″.

The Snyder Family

When Mary Snyder completed her crazy quilt in 1899, she had been married to Isaac Snyder for more than twenty-five years and had given birth to two sons, Charles, born June 12, 1873, and William, born September 16, 1878. The family farmed wheat and corn in Perry Township, Montgomery County, Ohio, for more than thirty years. Mary's widowed mother, Elizabeth Smith, also lived with the family.

As Mary stitched her quilt in 1898, twenty-six-year-old Charles was serving with the U.S. Infantry in Cuba. He was stationed near Santiago as a teamster but contracted malaria and spent almost the entire time in a hospital at Guantánamo. Because of this recurrent illness, Charles was discharged from the service after less than one year and settled in St. Louis, Missouri, to work as a clerk.

The quilt remained in the Snyder family until the early 1990s, when the last descendent sold it to a man in Trade, Tennessee, a small town near the North Carolina border. While vacationing in the area in 1993, Greg and Barri Brown acquired the Snyder Crazy Quilt, and it is now a cherished part of their quilt collection.

"Home Sweet Home" and "1.8.9.8" quilt blocks.

The Miller Crazy Quilt

Size: *84˝ x 91 ¹/₂ ˝*
Date: *1890*
Maker: *Alva Francis Miller*
           born: Echovale Peedee, Christian County Kentucky

The Miller Crazy Quilt

THE MILLER CRAZY QUILT is assembled from sixteen blocks, twelve measuring 18 by 18 inches, and four measuring 10 by 18 inches. The foundation fabric is white cotton, heavily sized.

The wide array of fabrics used includes silks, silk brocades, satins, velvets, and velveteens, as well as many grosgrain ribbons. A splendid variety of velvets is displayed, including ten assorted striped, eight different cut velvets, and several solids. The ribbon widths vary from $1^1/8$ to $4^3/4$ inches. The fabric patches were first basted to the foundation, then secured in place with decorative seam stitching. Characteristically, over time several of the fabric patches have become shredded or have deteriorated completely. The raw edges of the lightweight fabrics (silks, satins, etc.) were turned under, while the velvet edges were not. The corners of a few ribbons were turned back, revealing their undersides, with decorative stitching added around the edges.

The patches are abundantly embellished with motifs typical of the era, including stem-stitched outlines of a cat, bird, child, flowers, and a painted owl. There are embroidered chenille flowers, as well as family initials, names, and dates: "JM," "E," "F," "JAM," "JWW," "FM," "H Miller," "Harrie 1888," "Carl Miller 1889," "1842," and "1882." Individual silk and flocked flowers are secured to the quilt by buttonhole stitching around the petals. At the center of four blocks is a woven commemorative silk from a health exhibition showing four small children side by side in a three-wheel pram. Variations of the feather and cretan stitches were used to cover the seams on the individual blocks before they were joined together.

The quilt back is made of two panels of a deep-red polished cotton stitched together by sewing machine. The quilt is constructed without any batting; the top and back are tacked together with heavy red silk thread at approximately 10-inch intervals. The tacking is carefully hidden within the seams on the quilt top. The border is in excellent condition and is a beautiful soft moss-green velveteen, 8 inches wide, hand stitched in place with mitered corners. The quilt edges are hand stitched together, and a decorative red cord added around the entire quilt edge is stitched into a figure eight at the corners.

On this block note the appliquéd silk flower and ribbon with turned-down corner; the Miller Crazy Quilt, 1890, 84″ x 91¹/₂ ″.

The Miller Family

Born December 15, 1859, in Roaring Springs, Kentucky, Joseph Andrew Miller was twenty-two when he wed Alva Francis Coleman from Echovale Peedee, a small town several miles away, on October 4, 1882. The couple moved to Princeton, Kentucky, where Joseph, following in his father's footsteps as a medical doctor, set up his own practice. In addition to his busy medical practice, Joseph also was the district surgeon for the Illinois Central Railroad.

Joseph and Alva had four sons: Fulton, born in 1883; Hugh, in 1886; Harry, in 1888; and Karl Palmer, in 1889. It was after the birth of Karl that Alva stitched this crazy quilt, on which she embroidered the names and initials of her husband and young children as well as birthdates and the date of her marriage to Joseph. Alva died in 1894, leaving Joseph with four sons between the ages of five and eleven years.

In 1899 Joseph married Theodosia McCormick, a teacher and principal of the Princeton Collegiate Institute. The school offered primary, intermediate and college-level courses, ranging from mathematics, natural sciences, and language to music and art. Theodosia became a very positive influence on the boys as they matured. Fulton became a seaman; Hugh was killed in an explosion at a DuPont gunpowder plant in 1907; Harry became a chemist; and Karl became a Presbyterian minister.

Alva Miller's sons, clockwise from top left, Fulton, Hugh, Karl Palmer, and Harry, circa 1893.

Karl and his wife, Abby, had four children: Hugh, Joseph, Louise, and John Palmer. The Miller Crazy Quilt was passed down to Karl and Abby, then later given to Louise, who recalled that, during her childhood, the quilt was unpacked and displayed during holidays and special family occasions. In the early 1990s Louise gave the quilt to her brother John, the family historian.

John Palmer Miller also became a medical doctor and practiced family medicine in Newport Beach, California, where he and his wife, Eleanor, raised five children. It is expected that this family heirloom will be handed down to the next generation of the family for safekeeping.

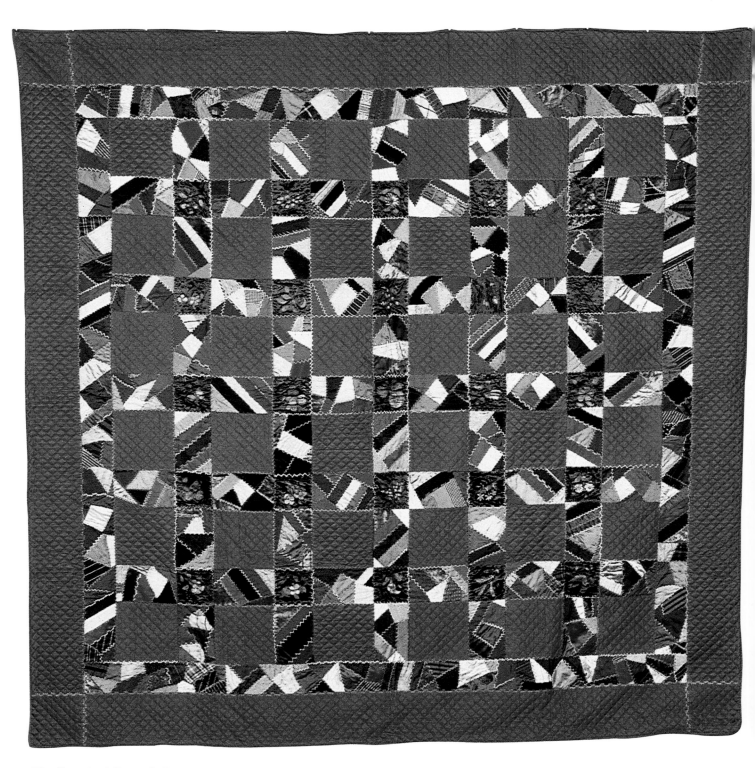

The Contained Crazy Quilt
Size: 73″ x 73″
Date: 1895–1900
Maker: Unknown

The Contained Crazy Quilt

THE CRAZY-PATCH BLOCKS in this quilt are confined to specific areas. There are thirty-six 6-by-6-inch blocks of red quilted satin, framed by sashes of crazy patches measuring 6 by 3 3/4 inches. A 3 3/4-inch solid black silk corner square with painted flowers joins the crazy-patch blocks where they intersect. The red satin fabric is a commercially manufactured and machine-quilted lining that was available for use in clothing.

Five different cotton fabrics comprise the foundation for the crazy-patch blocks, and a thin layer of batting separates the crazy patches and foundation fabric. The black silk squares also have a batting layer but do not have any foundation backing. The crazy patches were appliquéd through the batting onto the foundation, and then all the blocks were joined together with a running stitch.

The crazy-patch fabrics are primarily velvets and solid-colored silks, with a few brocades and ribbons. Flower motifs are painted on each black silk square for embellishment, and the decorative seam coverings are stitched with silk thread using variations of the feather and herringbone stitches. A 3 1/4-inch-wide crazy-patch border frames the inner blocks. A 5 1/2-inch-wide red quilted satin border completes this well-designed quilt.

The quilt back has a 46-inch center square of white cotton bordered by 13 1/2 inches of light-brown cotton, hand stitched together. The quilt back and top are tacked together with random hidden stitches. The quilt edge is finished in a matching red satin binding, hand stitched in place.

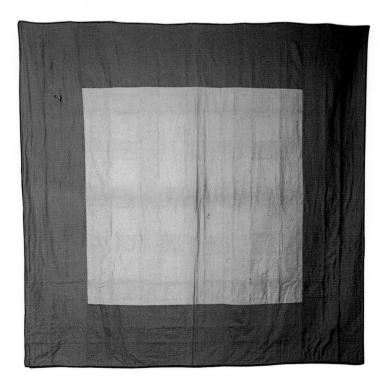

Back of the Contained Crazy Quilt, 1895–1900, 73˝ x 73˝.

Painted flowers highlight a black silk corner square that joins the crazy-patch blocks where they intersect.

Note the decorative seam coverings stitched with silk thread in variations of the feather and herringbone stitches.

The Fan Design

ALTHOUGH FANS were seen in quilts prior to the 1880s, they flourished during the Victorian Era and were often incorporated into crazy quilts. When the fan pattern was used overall in a quilt made from luxurious silks and velvets, it is recognized as being from the Victorian Era. After the decline in crazy quilt popularity, the fan design continued to be used as shown in the cotton scrap quilt made by my great grandmother (see the Carter Fan Quilt).

Fans incorporated into the Davis Crazy Quilt, 1892.

Fans incorporated into the Black on Black Crazy Quilt, 1994, at left, and the Family Signature Crazy Quilt, 1995.

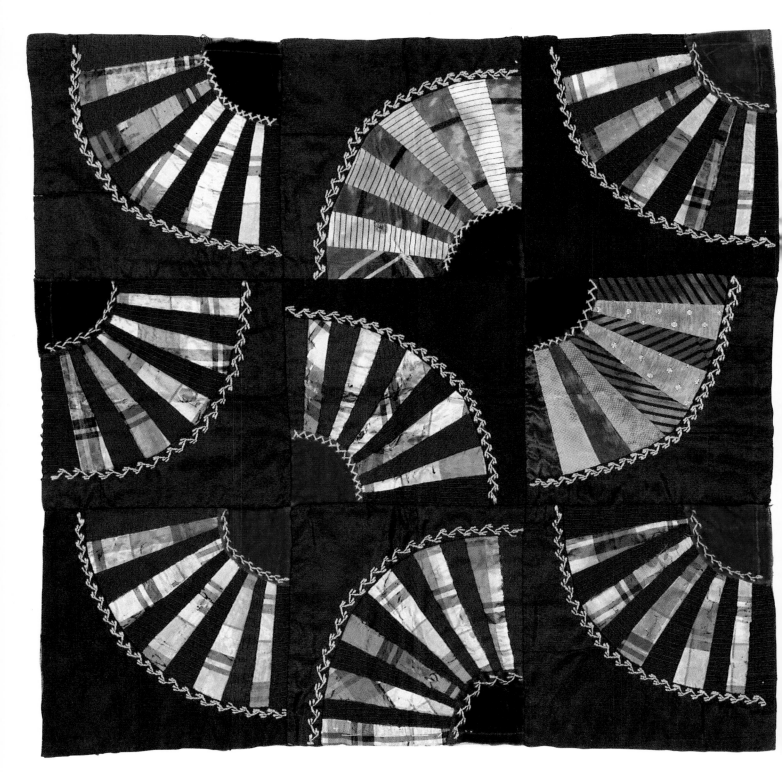

The Fan Blocks

Size: 15 ¾ ˝ x 15 ¾ ˝ section
Date: 1880s
Maker: Unknown

The Fan Blocks

THIS SECTION of nine blocks from a larger quilt is a good representation of a fan design from the Victorian Era. Each finished block measures 5 1/4 inches square. Three different brown cotton fabrics make up the foundation blocks. Each fan includes eleven silk and taffeta spokes, with maroon velvet for the fan base. On three blocks the dark backgrounds were pieced together with a variety of black fabrics. The fans are hand appliquéd, and the blocks are assembled with a running stitch, leaving a 1/4- to 3/8-inch seam allowance.

The decorative stitching is limited to a feather stitch along the velvet fan base and spoke top. Basting thread can still be found along one side of the blocks. The silk fabric in the fan spokes is brittle and crumbles easily.

Each fan block measures 5 1/4″ x 5 1/4″.

The G.M.S. Crazy Patch Fan Quilt
Size: 73″ x 73″
Date: 1888
Maker: Unknown, initials G.M.S.

The G.M.S. Crazy Patch Fan Quilt

THE BODY OF THIS FAN crazy quilt has seven rows, assembled from forty-nine blocks that each measure 9 x 9 inches. Fabrics used in the foundation include striped and plaid cottons, and lightweight and coarse heavy-weave muslins.

The fabric patches were hand pieced with brown thread and appliquéd to their foundation. Initially, a fan was stitched into the corner of each block; the spokes were stitched first, then the base and top border. The fan's base fabric, alternating spokes, and top border are black satins or silks. The colored spokes, in satin and brocades, are in muted shades of pink, blue, light brown, and warm sunlight yellow. Each fan's colored spokes are from the same fabric.

Once the fan was appliquéd in place, the remainder of the foundation block was covered with thirteen to twenty-one crazy patches. Fabrics used include silks, satins, brocades, polished cottons, and ribbons.

The decorative seam coverings were completed before the blocks were assembled. Solid-color silk thread as well as variegated silk in shades of yellow, gold, green, purple, and blue were used to stitch over the seams. Chenille or three-strand cotton floss also was used to cover a few seams. Although a decorative feather stitch covers many seams, straight-stitch combinations appear to make up the majority of the decorative stitches. The fan spokes do not have any decorative seam coverings.

Only two patches have embroidery—one with the initials "G.M.S.," the other with the date "1888"—and both were stitched using a stem stitch.

Once the decorative stitching was completed, the blocks were ready for assembling. We can only wonder how the maker came to put her blocks together, unaware of the error she was making. She assembled two rows of five blocks each into one section, placing the fan bases tip to tip against each row. She then stitched three sections together in a uniform manner, equaling six rows of blocks. With the fourth block section, instead of adding it to the edge of the previous quilt section, she stitched it to the top of these rows, breaking the continuity of her design. She placed the seventh and last row of blocks at the bottom edge of the quilt, not matching the fan motif in any particular manner. Decorative stitches were then added to the block seams.

The quilt is finished with a 5-inch-wide maroon velveteen border, hand stitched in place with mitered corners. The quilt was made without an inner layer of batting.

The back consists of two layers of cotton fabric machine stitched together in a crisscross quilting pattern. Three panels of this quilted backing were stitched together to fit the crazy quilt back. The quilt's outside border edges were turned inward and hand stitched together. The top and back were tacked together with small stitches.

Fan block sections measure 9″ x 9″. Note the initials G.M.S. in the blue satin patch; the G.M.S. Crazy Patch Fan Quilt, 1888, 73″ x 73″.

G.M.S. 1888

The story of this quilt is not so much about its maker as about its journey, which is the case with many crazy quilts. It is known that the maker's initials were G.M.S., as seen on the quilt, and that the quilt was created in 1888. The maker lived in the San Francisco Bay area all her life, and upon her death many years ago, her possessions were given to various family members. The crazy quilt moved from place to place and in the early 1990s made its way from relatives in San Francisco to a grand-niece in Fullerton, California.

The quilt arrived with an assortment of G.M.S.'s belongings, odds and ends unwanted by other family members. The grand-niece kept these belongings for several years before taking them to an antique consignment shop where they were sold. These items included several pieces of Depression-era glass, a cloisonné jar, table linens, and the crazy quilt.

Many crazy quilts make similar journeys; they are lovingly created, displayed, and admired, and then, with the passage of time, they become neglected and unappreciated. They are often stained, musty smelling, and in varying states of deterioration when they are finally discarded or sold in consignment and antique shops. Today, as we find and acquire these treasures, we can care for and protect them as well as admire and enjoy them.

The backing is machine-quilted cotton.

The Carter Fan Quilt
Size: *85″ x 61″*
Date: *1933–1934*
Maker: *Allie Minerva Carter*

The Carter Fan Quilt

THIS TWIN-BED QUILT is comprised of thirty-five fan pattern blocks, each measuring 8 1/2 by 8 1/2 inches. The blocks are machine pieced, then set on point. The fan spokes are made from cotton calico and shirting, and each fan base is pink cotton. Some fabrics are still very bright while others have faded noticeably.

There is a thin layer of batting between the quilt top and the white cotton backing. The layers are hand quilted, sixteen stitches per inch, along the fan seam lines. The quilt edge is finished with a manufactured pink seam binding that is hand stitched in place.

The Carter Family

In the early 1840s Allison Ellison Carter and his wife, Louisa, moved by wagon from Virginia to Paris, Tennessee, where Louisa bore twelve children, seven of whom survived. When the Carters' children were young, the family moved to Bloomfield, Missouri, to farm.

In 1861 their eighteen-year-old son, Radalphus, enlisted in the Missouri Cavalry, serving four years and fighting in the American Civil War. During the war a small skirmish was fought on the Carter farm, and an iron cannonball landed in one of the fields. That cannonball now sits in my mother's living room.

After the war, Radalphus married Louisa Ellen Barlett, whose family owned a large farm in Bloomfield. A short time later the entire Carter family left Bloomfield and helped found the town of Dexter, Missouri.

Once settled in Dexter, Radalphus and Louisa had ten children, two of whom died in infancy. Although Radalphus was much loved by everyone, he unfortunately was not a successful businessman, and so supported his large family by doing general hauling and drayage.

In the late 1880s their eldest son, Robert Orson Carter, married Allie Minerva Crits. The couple had three children, Wilson (born in 1895), Louise, and Neal. Robert opened the Dexter Retail Mercantile, a five-and-dime general store, which he operated for thirty-one years.

John Wesley McColgan, also of Dexter, married Della P. Biggerstaff on November 27, 1888. They had four daughters, Reba, Erie, Ruth (born March 17, 1898), and Lee. Homer, the McColgans' only son, died in infancy. The family's successful farm was situated several miles outside of Dexter, while their large home was located at the edge of town on a twelve-acre parcel. Della McColgan was a large and domineering woman and not very pleasant. She hated housework but loved her pet turkeys, which she allowed to roam throughout the house. Della taught her daughters how to skin squirrels, and apparently did not want any of her girls to marry.

In 1920 Wilson Carter and Ruth McColgan wished to marry, but Della was bitterly opposed to the union. Realizing that he and Ruth would have to move if they were wed, Wilson visited California to explore business opportunities. Ruth then went to her father to gain his consent, and Wilson and Ruth were married in the parlor of the McColgan home. Only family members attended the ceremony, but the bride and groom's friends gave them a send-off at the station as they boarded the train for California on their wedding night.

Wilson's father closed his general store and moved the entire Carter family to California to join

The Carter Family of Inglewood, California, Easter Sunday 1934. Standing, from left, Ruth Carter, Louise Carter Lion, and Mamma Carter. Front, from left, Wilson Carter, Frances Carter, and Robert O. Carter.

the newlyweds. Settling in Inglewood, Wilson and his father opened the Inglewood Book and Stationery Store, which they built into a successful business that was owned and operated by the family for fifty years.

Ruth and Wilson had two children, Robert, and my mother, Frances. Wilson's mother, known as Mamma Carter, was the quiltmaker in the family. My mother remembers as a child seeing Mamma Carter working on the fan quilt shown here about the time of the 1933 Long Beach earthquake. The store's plate-glass windows were shattered by the quake, and glass jars filled with ink fell from the shelves and broke, making a huge mess. The entire family pitched in to clean up the store, and it was sometime later that Mamma Carter finally finished the fan quilt.

This quilt has been used and washed often over the years, and I remember Grammie Ruth always kept it in the hall closet. When she passed away in 1987, I brought the quilt into my home.

The J. W. McColgan family lived in this home on Stoddard Street in Dexter, Missouri, from 1906 until 1961. A supermarket stands on the site today.

The Davis Crazy Quilt
Size: *48˝ x 57˝*
Date: *1892*
Maker: *Elizabeth Davis*
            born: 1838, Colorado

The Davis Crazy Quilt

THE DAVIS CRAZY QUILT consists of thirty blocks that measure approximately 10 by 10 inches and two blocks that measure 10 by 13 inches. The fabrics are an assortment of velvets, silk brocades, satins, and many ribbons. The ribbons are solid-color brocades and cut velvets, ranging from 1 1/2 to 3 1/4 inches wide. Two blocks are assembled from a variety of solid black fabrics.

This crazy quilt has a layer of fine soft batting sandwiched between the top fabric patches and foundation muslin. The crazy patches are basted through the batting to the foundation and then covered with embroidery and decorative stitches.

There are various embroidered motifs, including figures, flowers, oriental fan, butterfly, cat, owl, and the initial "B" for Bessie. There are also painted motifs, as well as chenille and silk-ribbon embroidery. Stitched into the quilt is a commemorative dance ribbon from the Marquette, Michigan, Lodge Quarter Century Celebration, dated January 15, 1883, and a printed silk from the Chicago, Milwaukee & St. Paul Railway, for which William Davis worked as an engineer. The seams are decoratively covered with numerous colors of silk thread in a wide variety of embroidery stitches. One corner of the crazy-quilt top was not completed, and it was never backed.

Chicago, Milwaukee & St. Paul Railway silk patch, the Davis Crazy Quilt, 1892, 48˝ x 57˝.

The Davis and Miller Families

Thomas Davis was born in 1836 and as a young man immigrated from Wales to Denver, Colorado. Thomas's wife, Elizabeth, bore their son, William, in 1869. Elizabeth stitched this crazy quilt as a wedding gift for William in the early 1890s when he married Bessie B. Fox.

While living in Blue Island, Illinois, John and Lucy Fox had three children: Emily, born in 1870; Arthur, in 1871; and Bessie, in 1874. John worked as a stone and coal dealer, while Lucy kept house and raised their three children with help from Mura Dircilo, a young Prussian servant girl.

In the early 1880s John Fox moved his young family to Denver, Colorado, where he had secured a better job. Emily married a Mr. Danks, while Bessie married William Davis, an engineer for the Chicago, Milwaukee & St. Paul Railway. Several years later Mr. Danks died, leaving Emily, who never remarried or had children. Emily moved in with Bessie and William, who also were childless, and the three lived together well into their eighties.

Arthur moved from Denver to San Francisco, where he worked as a banker. He married Louise Robertson, and they had two daughters, Evelyn, born in 1895, and Gladys, born three years later. After the 1906 San Francisco earthquake and subsequent fire that destroyed the bank where Arthur worked, the family moved to Arizona.

In 1914 Evelyn married George Wescott Miller, a traveling automobile-tire salesman. They made their home in Oakland, California, where they raised two sons, George

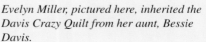

Evelyn Miller, pictured here, inherited the Davis Crazy Quilt from her aunt, Bessie Davis.

Jr. and Dudley Fox Miller. Dudley, after serving in the Philippines during World War II and graduating from college, married Frances Ruth Carter in 1950 and raised their family in the Los Angeles area.

Emily, William, and Bessie passed away during the 1950s, and their niece, Evelyn Miller, my grandmother, inherited the crazy-quilt top. In 1962 Evelyn gave it to my mother, Frances Miller. After storing the top for almost twenty-five years, my mother decided to complete the missing corner and have the quilt backed. She stitched a small piece of needlepoint for the corner and added her initials and the date, "FRM 1989." The quilt was then backed and bound with maroon velveteen, and tied. I treasure this crazy quilt because it connects my family's past with the present. Eventually, it will be given to my daughters for continued love and care.

The Carr Crazy Quilt
Size: 58″ x 70″
Date: 1884–1888
Maker: Lottie and Lois Carr

The Carr Crazy Quilt

LOTTIE CARR and her daughter, Lois, began stitching this crazy quilt in March 1884. The fabric patches were first basted and then appliquéd onto foundation blocks of heavy blue cotton or white muslin. The basting threads were never removed from many of these patches. The blocks measure 15 by 15 inches, 6 by 30 inches, 5 by 15 inches, and 24 by 22 inches. Sometimes smaller blocks were appliquéd into the larger blocks. Once the blocks were assembled, additional patches were appliquéd over several seams to hide them.

The fabrics in the quilt include plaid and striped silks, a few brocades, and velveteen in maroon, black, and shades of brown. Many ribbons in soft brown, black, maroon, blues, greens, cream, and shades of red are seen throughout. The most prized fabric on the quilt is a patch of cream-colored satin which came from Queen Victoria's palace in England. The fabric, from the queen's redecorated rooms, was sent to Lois by a cousin who was employed at the palace. Lois embroidered a gold crown onto the patch in honor of England's longest-reigning monarch.

On the quilt flowers are embroidered using lazy daisy, stem, and satin stitches. A new moon with stars and a lady's shoe are appliquéd onto patches with a buttonhole stitch. There are several butterflies embroidered in chenille and silk thread, accented with gold metallic chenille. An unusual twelve-legged spider is embroidered in the middle of a spiderweb, and a bird perched on a tree branch is outlined in a stem stitch. The quilt took four and a half years to complete, as evidenced by the dates "March 1884," "1885," "1886," "1887," and "Sept. 1888." The embroidered initials are "LMC," for Lottie Carr, and "LGC," for her daughter, Lois. The "C" is stitched at an angle.

Two of the three commemorative ribbons on the quilt are from the Independent Order of Odd Fellows (I.O.O.F.), a men's organization. The third ribbon represents President Garfield: "Our Hero, James A. Garfield, Born Nov. 19, 1831, Shot July 2, 1881, and Died Sept. 19, 1881."

The decorative seam coverings are stitched in solid and variegated colors of silk thread, with an occasional seam covered in stranded floss. Most of the stitches seen are herringbone, feather, straight, and lazy daisy. It is apparent from the contrast in size and evenness of the stitches that two people worked on the quilt.

A 5-inch-wide light-brown velveteen border is hand stitched in place, with the seam covered in green feather stitching and accented with a red lazy daisy. The entire border is painted in a variety of alternating large and small flower motifs, with roses in each corner.

This crazy quilt was not originally backed and has never had any batting. In 1977 Lois's niece, Hazel Weech, backed the quilt with a bed sheet, machine stitching the edges together. Except for a few deteriorating patches, this quilt is in excellent condition.

James Garfield commemorative ribbon; the Carr Crazy Quilt, 1884–1888, 58˝ x 70˝.

The satin fabric with embroidered gold crown came from Queen Victoria's palace.

The Carr Family

In 1865 Ezra and Lottie Carr's first daughter, Lois, was born. While Lois was a toddler, Ezra moved his young family from Minnesota to Russell Gulch, Colorado, where on May 17, 1871, their second daughter, Edna Josephine, was born, followed by Lillian and Beryl. The family later settled in Boulder, Colorado, where Ezra farmed and the girls attended school. Lottie taught her daughters sewing skills at home, and when Lois was nineteen, she and her mother gathered scraps of fabric together and began working on the crazy quilt shown here. During the four and a half years it took them to complete the quilt, crazy quilting was at the height of its popularity.

About the time the covering was completed, Lois met John Hazelton, a young man four years her junior. Lottie

Members of the Carr family shown in this photograph taken in the late 1930s include, standing, from left, June Booth, Hazel Weech, Bernice Booth, Ezra H. Booth, Walter Booth, Charlie Purmort, Edith Carr Lewis, and Lois Carr Hazelton. Seated, from left, are Shirley Jean Booth, Edna Carr Booth, Monica Kay Mercer, and Beryl Carr Purmort.

never cared for John but, much to her dismay, Lois and John were married in 1890. They had two sons, Oscar, born in 1892, and Eber, born fifteen years later. At times John had difficulty supporting his family and the young couple was forced to live with Lois's parents. Lottie was never happy with this arrangement and thought that John did not work hard enough. Eventually, around 1910, John moved his family from the Carr home in Boulder to Bellevue, Idaho, where he was employed by the telephone company as an electrician.

On December 5, 1892, Lois's sister, Edna Josephine, married Walter Booth, who was born on a farm in Spring Valley, Iowa, November 12, 1869. In 1881 his parents, Horace and Mary, left their Iowa farm and moved the family in a covered wagon pulled by oxen to Boulder, Colorado, where Horace continued farming. Walter took a job in the city driving a horse-drawn streetcar and for a short time worked as a typesetter on the city's first newspaper. Edna kept house and gave birth to Hazel in 1884, and Ezra in 1903. In 1908, after working in the city for sixteen years, Walter moved the family to Bellevue and then Meridian, Idaho, where he farmed for the next twenty-nine years. In 1937 Edna and Walter retired in Nampa, Idaho, where they lived until their deaths in 1954 and 1956, respectively.

When Lois's husband, John Hazelton, passed away, she was ill with respiratory problems and could not manage alone during the harsh winters. As a result, she moved to Edna and Walter's home where she lived until her death in 1939. Lois always cherished her crazy quilt and kept it in her possession, for it represented a special time she had spent with her mother. Family members recall how proud Lois was of her quilt and how very special the Queen Victoria satin fabric patch was to her.

Edna inherited her sister's treasured crazy quilt and eventually passed it on to her married daughter, Hazel Weech. Hazel also lived in Nampa and operated a dress shop until her husband, Jim, passed away. She then moved to Seal Beach, California, to be near her children. For years Hazel's granddaughter-in-law, Darlene Hoadley, admired the crazy quilt, but Hazel could not be persuaded to let it go. Finally, in 1977, when Hazel was eighty-three years old, she was willing to part with the quilt. Darlene's husband, Jim, knowing how much Darlene loved the crazy quilt, arranged to give it to her for Christmas. Jim gave his Gramma Weech one hundred dollars for the quilt and asked her to sew a back on it, which she did.

Since 1977 the crazy quilt has been in Darlene's home, draped over the back of her bed, and in time she will pass it on to her daughter, Wendy.

Part 11

Instructions

Fabrics: silk, satins, and ribbons.

Fabrics

VICTORIAN ERA crazy quilts were predominately constructed from silks, satins, velvets, brocades, and ribbons. Sometimes quilts were made from wool fabrics alone or from a combination of silks and satins. Today there are many wonderful fabrics available in yardage shops to give crazy quilts a rich and luxurious look. An excellent source for silk is the Kirk Collection (see Resources), which offers fabrics that may be purchased by mail.

Lace and embellishments will also give a Victorian look to your contemporary crazy quilt, and a personal touch may be added by including commemorative ribbons or family photo-to-fabric transfers (see Resources).

The silk fabrics in these four 1930s 12˝ x 12˝ crazy-patch blocks appeared to be in good condition, but began to tear when handled. I recommend using new fabrics in your crazy quilt.

Each of these Victorian Fan foundation blocks from the 1880s measures 5 ¹/₂″ x 5 ¹/₂″.

Note the different fabrics used to make the foundation blocks.

Five different foundation fabrics were used on the crazy-patch block sections of the Contained Crazy Quilt, stitched in 1885.

Foundations

THE FOUNDATION fabric gives the crazy quilt its base and acts as a stabilizer when embroidering on delicate fabric patches.

1. For a foundation use muslin fabric or a soft, clean white sheet (not an old one that could tear or shred). Cut a foundation piece approximately 8 to 12 inches larger than the finished dimensions of the crazy-patch area to provide room for the embroidery hoop to grasp when stitching embroidery on the patch. I construct my crazy quilts on a single foundation, but you may wish to assemble yours from blocks, appropriately sizing the foundation to fit each block. Stitching one block at a time makes it easy to carry your needlework with you while away from home.

2. Place the foundation fabric on a flat surface and use a permanent fabric-marking pen to draw an outline of the area to be covered with a crazy patch. Turn the foundation over and trace the outline on the back. This line will be basted later. (See Figure 1.)

3. Begin piecing the patches from a top corner of the foundation, working down and out. (See Figure 1.)

4. To create a fabric patch seam allowance (at least ½ inch), fold the fabric edge over a template and iron. Place the folded edge of the patch over an adjoining patch in the desired position and pin in place with one or two pins. The seam allowances of both patches will be trimmed later. At the border, piece 1 inch over the crazy-patch outline. (See Figure 2.)

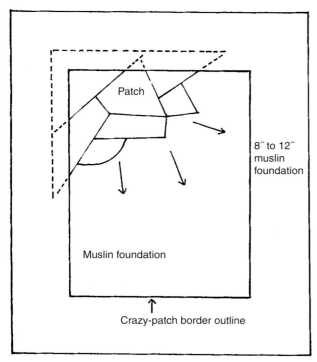

Figure 1.

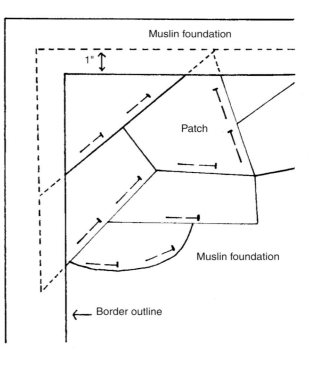

Figure 2.

The foundation fabrics in the Snyder Crazy Quilt, 1899, were taken from heavy clothing.

Helpful Hints

- Balance color and texture by making several patches from the same fabric and distributing them evenly throughout the quilt. Consider separating plaids, stripes, or prints with solid colors, allowing embroidery and decorative stitches to stand out.

- Do not leave patches pinned to a foundation longer than a day or two before appliquéing. Pins may leave permanent holes in some fabrics.

- When appliquéing a light patch over a dark patch, check to see that the seam allowance of the light patch is wide enough to cover the dark fabric underneath to prevent it from showing through.

- For a smoother seam when using velvet, iron the velvet pile seam allowance flat, then appliqué adjoining patches over the flattened pile.

Appliquéing

Basted border outline and trimed edge.

1. Before appliquéing the fabric patches, carefully lift each patch and trim any excess seam allowance, leaving approximately $1/2$ inch. This will make the quilt top as smooth and flat as possible.

2. Repin each patch securely into its original position and then appliqué to the foundation. Appliqué patches at the border edge 1 inch past the border outline.

3. When the top is completely stitched in place, turn the whole piece over to the back and, using thread of a contrasting color, baste along the traced outline. This basted line will indicate the border edge on the quilt top.

4. Trim to 1 inch any excess fabric outside the border edge. Note: Do not trim the foundation. To keep the fabrics from fraying around the outside border edge, apply Dritz® Fray Check™.

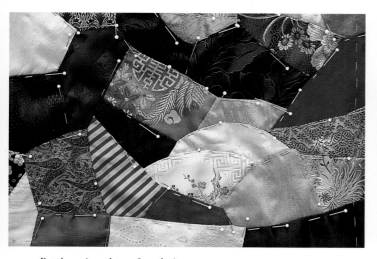

Patches pinned to a foundation.

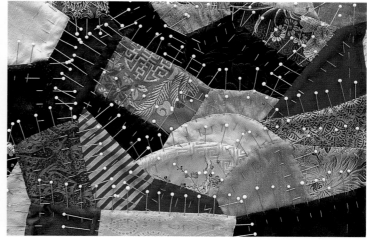

Seam allowances should be trimmed and patches repinned before being appliquéd in place.

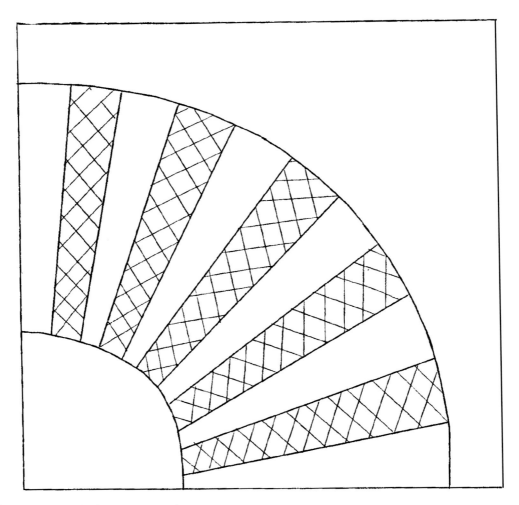

1880s Victorian Fan

5 ¼″ block; pattern shown at 90 percent of actual size

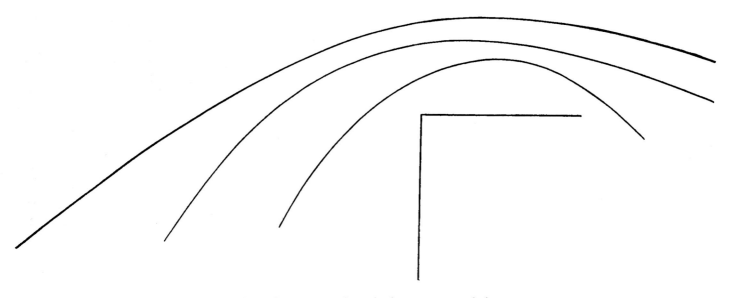

Template edge outlines; cut templates from poster board; shown at actual size

Templates cut from poster board.

Fan on the Carr Crazy Quilt, 1888.

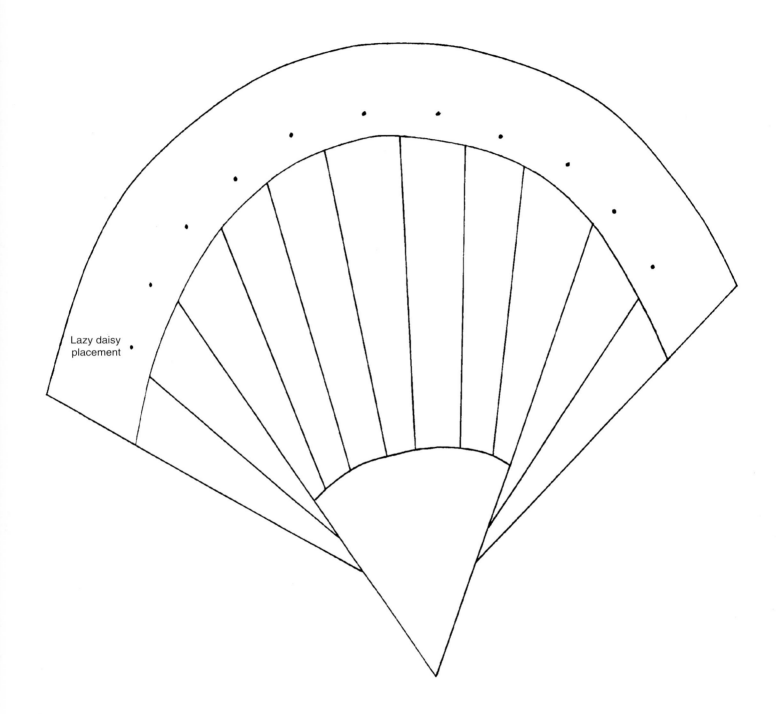

Lazy daisy
placement

Fan pattern from the Carr Crazy Quilt

Full-size pattern

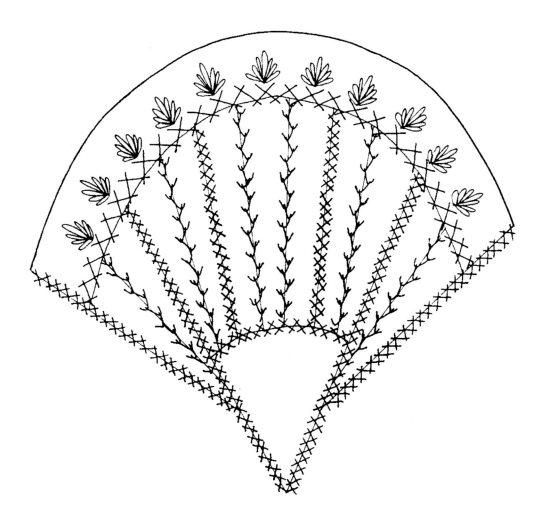

Stitch Guide

 a: Lazy daisy stitch

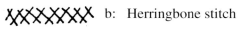 b: Herringbone stitch

 c: Feather stitch

Embroidered Patches

THROUGH THE AGES embroidery has given needleworkers an avenue to display their skills and artistic expression. On crazy quilts, it is the artistry of the embroidery and the arrangement of shapes and colors that make each quilt unique and personal.

The same embroidered motif often can be found on old crazy quilts from different regions of the country. In many cases this is because such motifs originated in widely distributed women's magazines that included design outlines which could be transferred and stitched on quilts. These antique quilt motifs can be reproduced on the quilts we create today, and you can draw inspiration from contemporary needle-art books and magazines. Other motifs you may wish to include are family signatures, initials, dates, places, pets, children's book characters, or any motif that has personal significance.

Embroidered Motifs Using the Transfer Paper Method

1. Choose the desired fabric patch and a motif to embroider onto it. If necessary, use a photocopy machine to reduce or enlarge the motif to fit the patch size.

2. With a pencil, trace the motif onto tracing paper.

3. Position the traced motif on the patch and hold it in place with a single piece of Scotch™ tape.

4. To transfer the motif, insert a sheet of Saral® transfer paper under the traced motif and use a pencil or pen to trace the motif's outline onto the patch. Carefully remove the tape, the traced motif, and the transfer paper from the patch, being careful not to smudge the transfer paper onto surrounding fabric patches.

5. Carefully secure the area to be stitched in an embroidery hoop. Embroider the motif, using one strand of Kreinik Soie D'Alger silk floss or DMC cotton floss.

Using transfer paper, trace pumpkins onto fabric.

Embroider pumpkins using long and short stitches.

BELOW: *Pumpkins on the Family Signature Crazy Quilt, 1995.*

Full-size pumpkins motif

Additional Motifs Using the Transfer Paper Method

Peacock adapted from wallpaper design

This 1990 reproduction of a 1930s Shand Kydd Frieze by Crown Wall Coverings was hand blocked and stenciled.

Helpful Hints

- If a transfer line is too heavy, use a piece of removable tape to lightly pat the transfer line to lighten it.
- If a transfer line begins to fade, use a sharpened chalk pencil to retrace the fading line.
- When you are not stitching, always remove the embroidery hoop so it will not leave a permanent crease in the fabric.
- Do not pull embroidery stitches too tight; doing so may cause the fabric patch to wrinkle or pucker.

Embroidered peacock adapted from the 1930s Shand Kydd Frieze stitched on a crazy-patch vest.

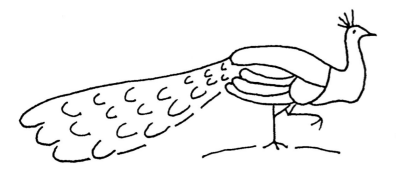

Full-size peacock adapted from wallpaper

RIGHT: *Peacock feather stitched in long and short stitch.*

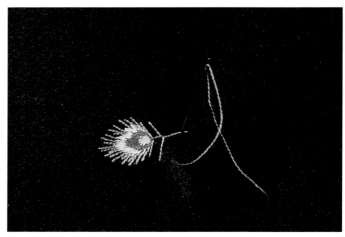

DFM monogram

As a wedding gift, my mother gave my father a pair of monogrammed gold cuff links. I photocopied the monogram and then transferred it onto a crazy patch.

DFM monogrammed cuff link.

1. To create this motif, photocopy the monogram and enlarge to the desired size.
2. Trace the initials onto tracing paper, then transfer onto desired patch.
3. Embroider the initials using a satin stitch.
4. Finish embroidering all the patch motifs before stitching the decorative seam coverings.

Use a satin stitch to embroider initials.

RIGHT: *Embroidered DFM monogram on the Family Signature Crazy Quilt, 1995.*

Quilt top in progress.

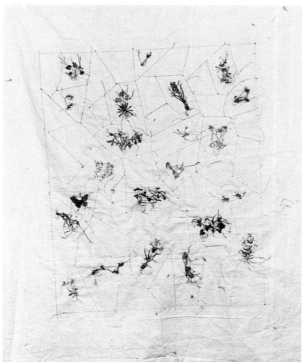

Foundation back.

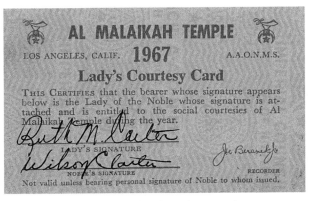

Original signatures of Ruth M. Carter and Wilson E. Carter, 1967.

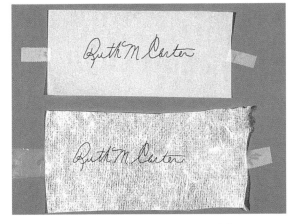

Trace the signature onto tracing paper and then onto rice paper.

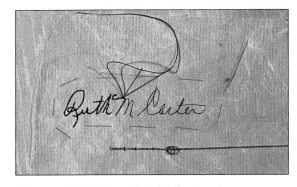

Use a couch stitch to embroider the signature.

Embroidered Motifs Using the Rice Paper Method

Rice paper may be found in many better art supply stores. I came upon rice paper sold as gift wrap in a craft store. If rice paper is not available, use the transfer paper method.

Signatures

1. Trace an original signature onto tracing paper. If necessary, use a photocopy machine to reduce or enlarge the motif to fit the desired patch size.
2. Place a piece of rice paper over the traced signature. The signature should show through the rice paper. Carefully outline the signature using a Pigma Micron permanent fabric pen, size 005 or 01.
3. Place the patch to be embroidered in an embroidery hoop. Position the rice-paper signature on the patch and baste in place.
4. Embroider the signature with a couch stitch using Kreinik Soie Gobelins silk, DMC pearl cotton #12, or one strand of DMC cotton floss. Couch only enough of the signature to hold its shape in place.
5. Carefully trim away the rice paper surrounding the couched signature and use tweezers to gently remove the remaining rice paper and any paper fibers.
6. Using the original signature as a visual guide, go back over the signature with additional couch stitches to completely secure it in place.

Ruth M. Carter and Wilson E. Carter embroidered signatures on the Family Signature Crazy Quilt, 1995.

Additional Motifs Using the Rice Paper Method

Rice paper may be used to embroider motifs following the basic instructions for signatures. Embroider the motif, using the appropriate stitches to cover the rice paper, then remove the remaining rice paper from around the motif edges.

Duck motif

Photocopy of pen and ink drawing.

One duck traced onto tracing paper.

Pen and ink drawing sketched by my father, Dudley Fox Miller, in 1950.

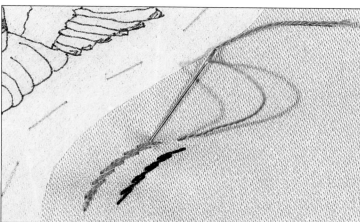

Stem stitch.

Duck stitched on rice paper using the stem stitch.

RIGHT: *Embroidered duck on the Family Signature Crazy Quilt, 1995.*

The Roosevelt Bears

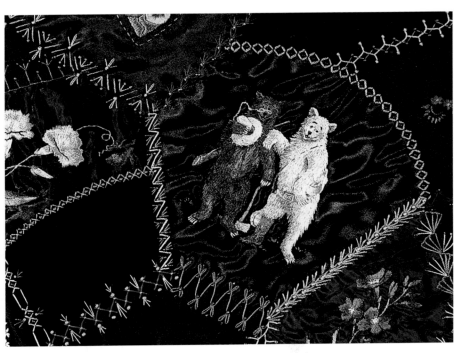

Teddy-B and Teddy-G, the Roosevelt Bears from The Traveling Bears in the East and West *by Seymour Eaton, 1905.*

The embroidered Roosevelt Bears using the rice paper method.

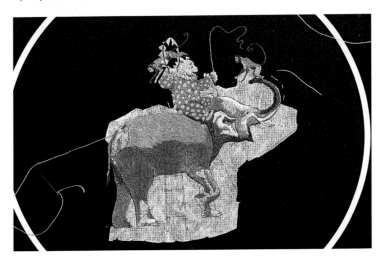

The Roosevelt Bears celebrate the Fourth from More About Teddy B. and Teddy G. The Roosevelt Bears Being Volume Two Depicting their further Travels and Adventures *by Seymour Eaton, 1907.*

Teddy-G riding a circus elephant stitched on rice paper. (See the Roosevelt Bear Crazy Quilt.)

The embroidered bears celebrating the Fourth of July stitched on the Family Signature Crazy Quilt, 1995.

Embroidery Motifs

The motifs on the following pages are from the Davis, Miller, Carr, and Snyder Crazy Quilts. These motifs are shown full size.

Good Luck horseshoe

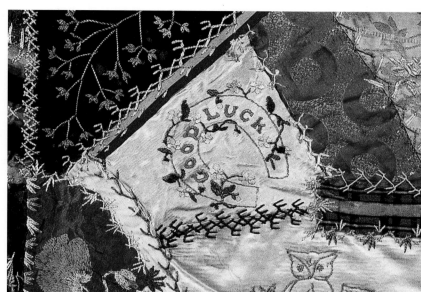

Good Luck horseshoe, Davis Crazy Quilt, 1892

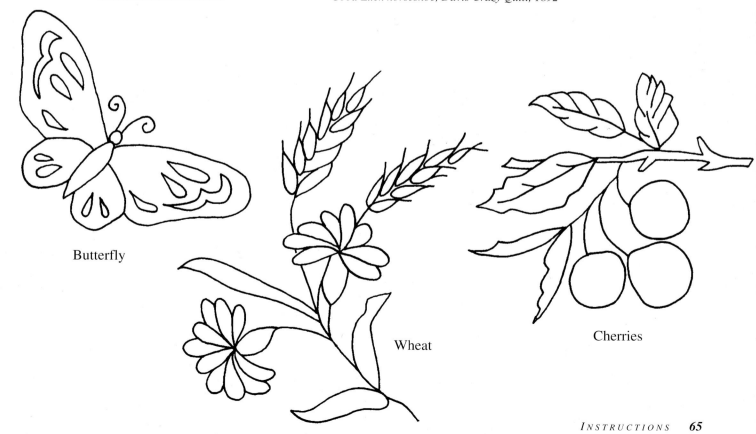

Butterfly

Wheat

Cherries

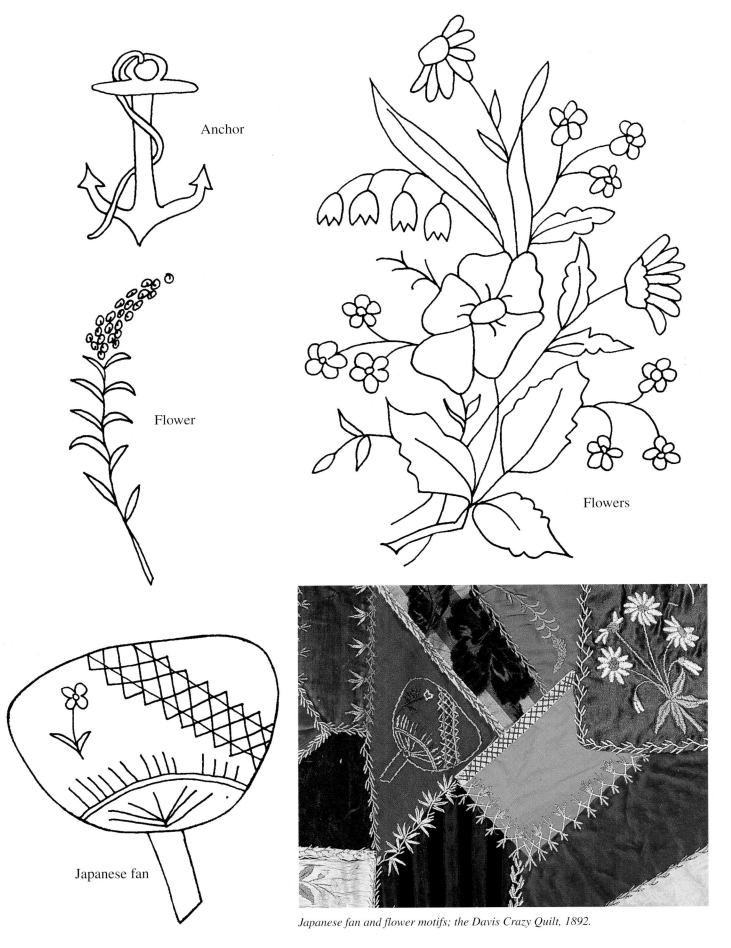

Anchor

Flower

Flowers

Japanese fan

Japanese fan and flower motifs; the Davis Crazy Quilt, 1892.

Mother and baby owl

Owl motif outlined in stem stitch; the Davis Crazy Quilt, 1892.

Cherries

Painted owl motif; the Miller Crazy Quilt, 1890.

Cat

Embroidered owl motif, 1997.

Daisy flowers

*Several motifs on the Davis Crazy Quilt, 1892. The daisies
are stitched in chenille and silk ribbon.*

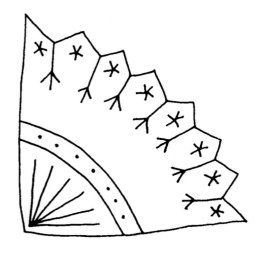

Fan

Small flower

Little girl feeding chicken

A little girl feeding a chicken, stitched in a stem stitch; the Davis Crazy Quilt, 1892.

Old woman

Old woman outlined in a stem stitch; the Davis Crazy Quilt, 1892.

Old woman outlined in a stem stitch; Jennifer's Crazy Quilt, 1992.

Little girl shielding her eyes from the wind, outlined in a stem stitch; the Miller Crazy Quilt, 1890.

Little girl shielding her eyes from the wind

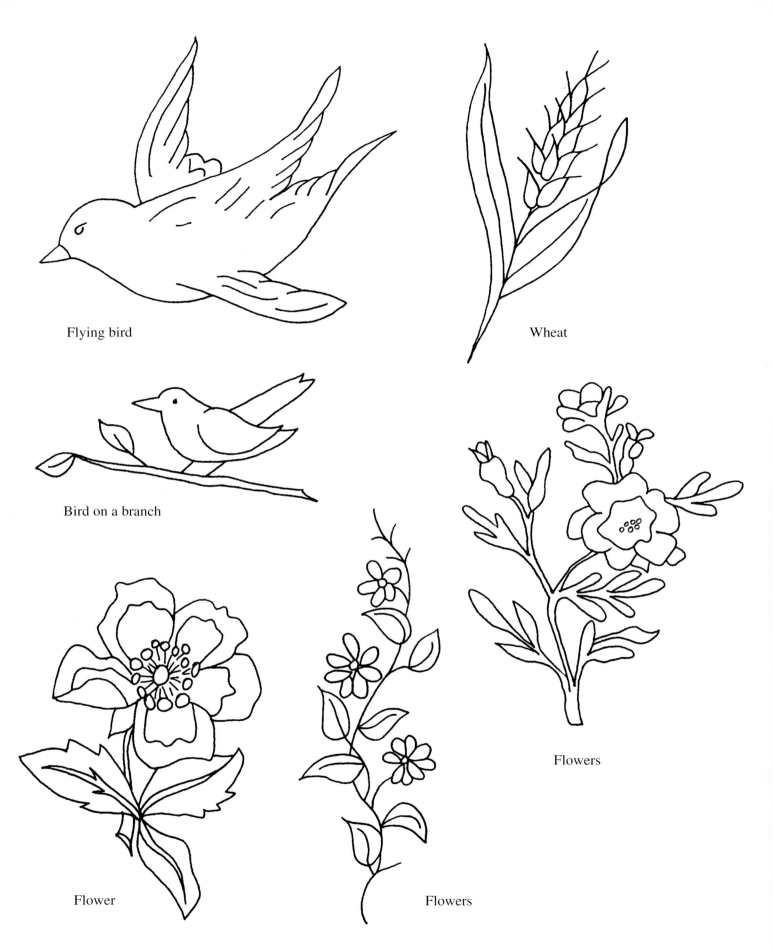

Flying bird

Wheat

Bird on a branch

Flower

Flowers

Flowers

Lady's shoe with leaves

Lady's shoe; the Carr Crazy Quilt, 1888.

Little girl wearing a bonnet

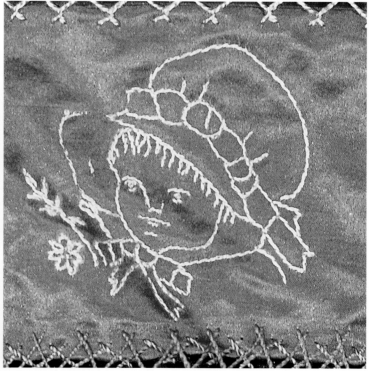

From left, the Miller Crazy Quilt, 1890, and the Davis Crazy Quilt, 1892. The girl in a bonnet was stitched in a stem stitch on both quilts.

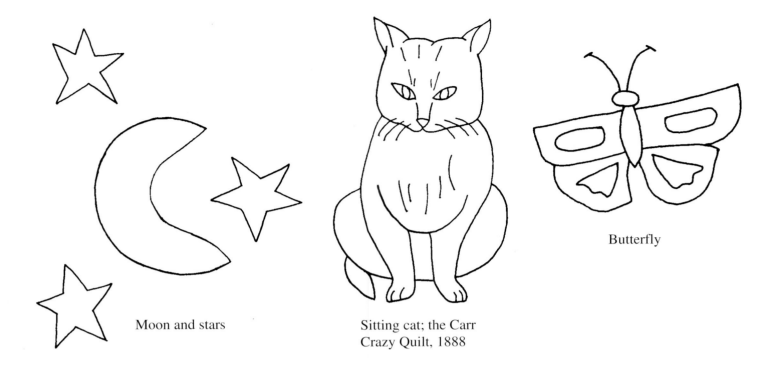

Moon and stars

Sitting cat; the Carr
Crazy Quilt, 1888

Butterfly

Flower and bird motif; the Snyder Crazy Quilt, 1899.

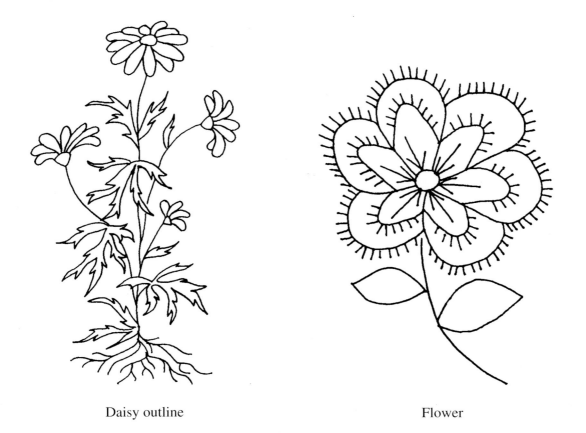

Daisy outline   Flower

Bird

Contemporary Motifs

Tree with bird's nest

Tree with bird's nest; Hearts and Flowers Crazy Quilt, 1996.

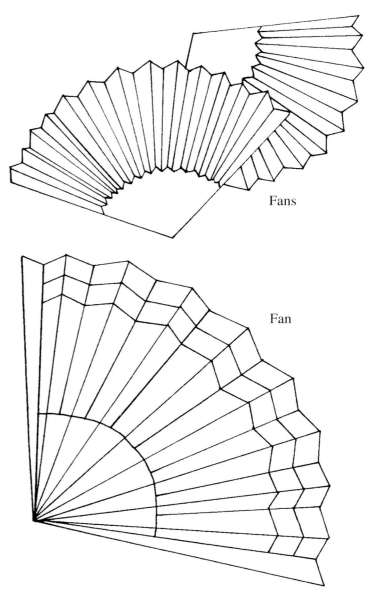

Fans

Fan

Daisies stitched in long and short stitches

Peacock

Peacock

Embroidered peacock; Hearts and Flowers Crazy Quilt, 1996.

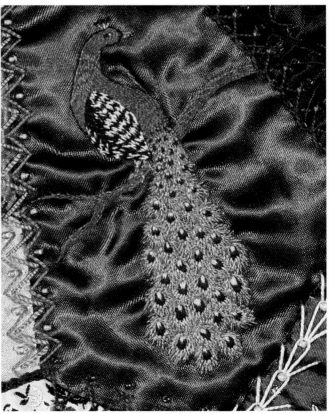

Embroidered peacock; Family Signature Crazy Quilt, 1995.

Berries stitched in long and short and satin stitches.

Berries

Peacock feather

Flower Heart

Heart

Basket

Flower heart in long and short stitches, satin stitch, and French knots.

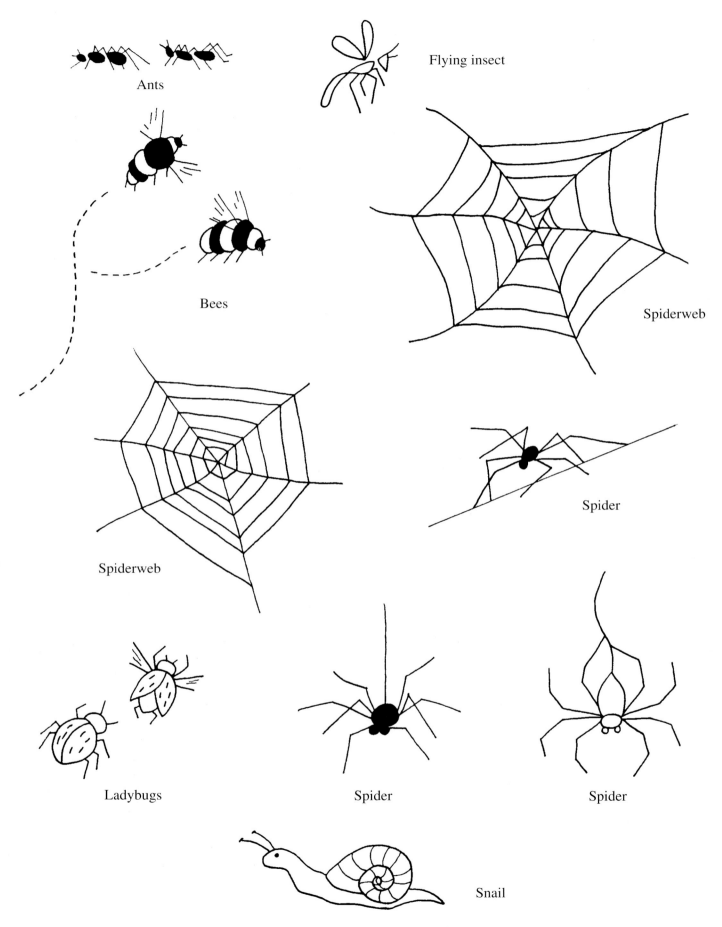

Ants

Flying insect

Bees

Spiderweb

Spiderweb

Spider

Ladybugs

Spider

Spider

Snail

Silk Ribbon Notes

SILK RIBBON EMBELLISHMENT on a crazy patch gives a delicate look that is very effective. Keep the silk ribbon stitches small and simple so they will hold their shape as the quilt is handled. Use a needle with a large eye so the silk ribbon will pass easily through the fabric; if the needle is too small, the ribbon will stress and fray when pulled through the fabric. Be sure the ribbon is not twisted but kept straight and flat for a neat stitch. Use transfer paper to outline your design onto the crazy patch.

Basket of Flowers; Family Signature Crazy Quilt, 1995.

Basket of Flowers; the Movie Crazy Quilt, 1994.

Straight stitch (daisies – golden yellow; leaves – forest green)

French knots (white flower centers – bright yellow; daisy centers – rust; flower centers – French knots, wrap around the needle once; large French knots – periwinkle, wrap around the needle twice)

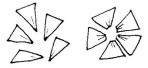

Loop stitch (large flowers – white; looped flowers – aqua)

Bullion stitch (pink DMC cotton floss; see Stitches)

Ribbon rose (rose center – dark apricot; outer rose – light apricot)

Feather stitch (light green DMC cotton floss; see Stitches)

Petite beads for accent (light green)

Basket of Flowers outline; the Movie Crazy Quilt, 1995

Stitch guide: The large white flowers are stitched in 7-millimeter silk ribbon. All other flowers and leaves are stitched in 4-millimeter silk ribbon (see Resources).

SILK RIBBON STITCHES

Securing the silk ribbon in the needle's eye

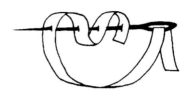

Knotting the silk ribbon end

Loop stitch

Loop stitch

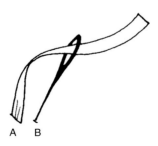

Loop stitch

Loop stitch

Straight stitch

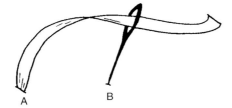

French knot

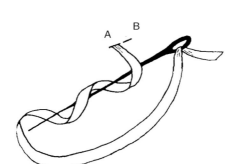

Ribbon rose

Thread spokes

Starting at point A, weave ribbon
around thread spokes

Decorative Seam Coverings

ON CRAZY QUILTS most decorative stitches are built upon several basic stitches, which can be simple or very elaborate. I study the decorative seam coverings on old crazy quilts for new or different stitches to incorporate into my quilts. To add depth to seam coverings, stitch them with several different size threads.

The seams on this quilt are covered in a fine twine and accented with red yarn; the Snyder Crazy Quilt, 1899.

Base stitches: Kreinik Soie Perlee: a 3-ply twisted filament silk yarn, DMC pearl cotton #5 or #8.

Accent stitches: Kreinik Soie Gobelins: a 2-ply twisted filament silk yarn, DMC pearl cotton #12, or DMC cotton floss.

Quilt border and edges: Kreinik Silk Serica™: a 3-ply filament silk or DMC pearl cotton #3.

Seams are covered in a herringbone stitch with variegated silk thread; the Southwick Crazy Quilt, 1898.

Both quilts' decorative seam coverings are stitched in silk thread; the Davis Crazy Quilt, 1892, and the Miller Crazy Quilt, 1890.

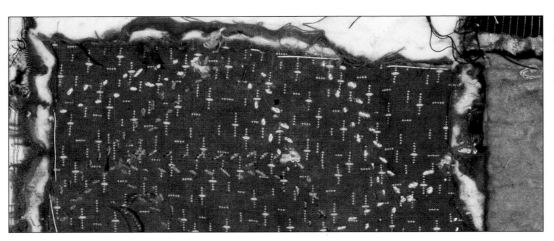

After 100 years the silk thread on the Contained Crazy Quilt's foundation is still vibrant.

A Note on Needles

It is important to use a needle with an eye large enough for the thread to pass easily through it. If your threaded needle is hard to pull through the fabric, the needle eye is too small for your thread.

To embroider: Embroidery needle sizes 1–9.
Bullion stitch or French knot: Milliner's needle sizes 3–10.
Silk ribbon embroidery: Chenille needle sizes 18–22.
Beading: Quilting Between size 10 or 12.

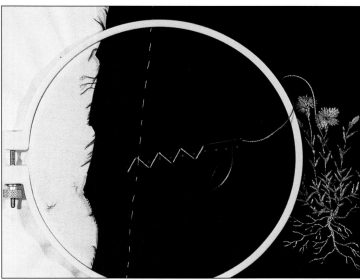

1. Using a chalk pencil and a ruler, mark the seam in equal increments every $1/4$ inch or 1 centimeter.
2. Place the area to be stitched into an embroidery hoop.
3. Using a stab stitch, first sew the base stitch, followed by the accent stitch, leaving a space about $1/8$ inch for a bead or French knot. Finish all stitching which requires use of an embroidery hoop before embellishing with beads.

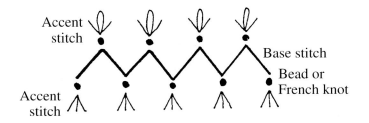

Accent stitch

Accent stitch

Base stitch

Bead or French knot

4. When covering a border edge seam, continue the decorative stitching $1/4$ to $1/2$ inch past the basted border line.

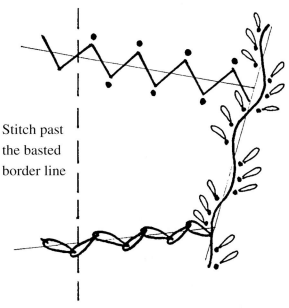

Stitch past the basted border line

Helpful Hints

• When several crazy-patch seams come together forming a continuous line, try to keep the decorative stitches uniform in height.

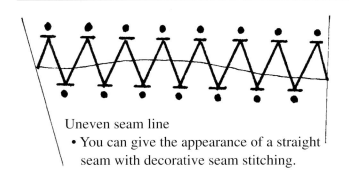

Uneven seam line

• You can give the appearance of a straight seam with decorative seam stitching.

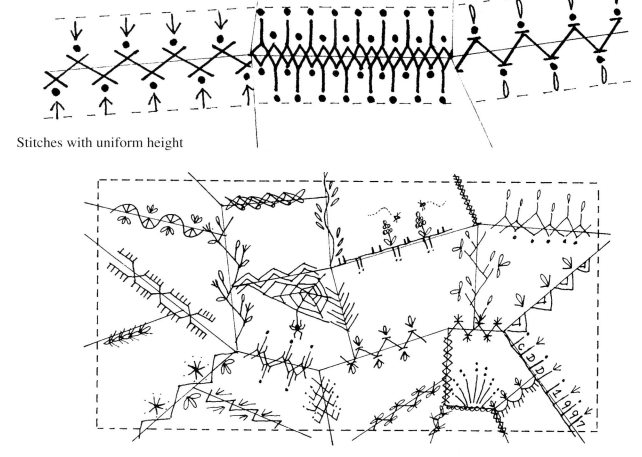

Stitches with uniform height

• On paper draw a diagram of the crazy quilt showing various decorative stitches. This saves a great deal of time and insures that the same or similar stitches are not placed too closely together.
• Do not remove the chalk marks after stitching; they eventually will fade.

Decorative Seam Stitches

THE MAJORITY of decorative seam covering stitches are combinations of a few basic stitches. Simple to very elaborate seam coverings may be created from these stitches.

Black on Black Crazy Quilt, 1995.

THE BASICS

Straight stitch

 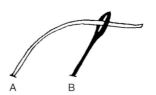

Chevron stitch

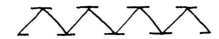

  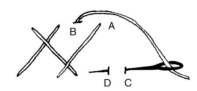 

Herringbone stitch

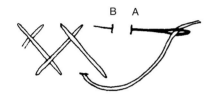

Cretan stitch

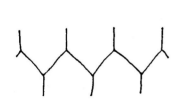 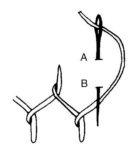 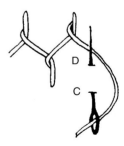

Buttonhole stitch

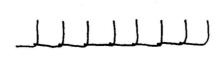 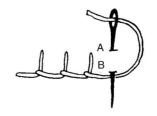

Feather stitch

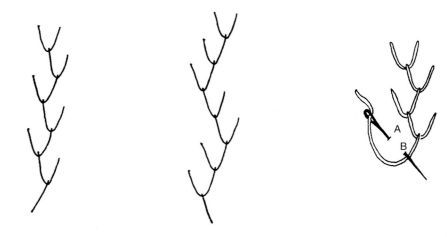

Fly stitch

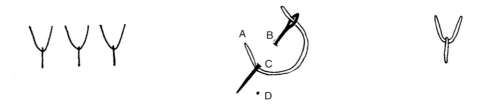

Stem stitch

Lazy daisy stitch

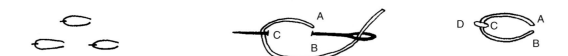

Chain stitch

 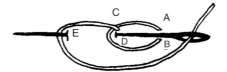

Couch stitch

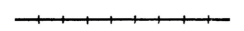 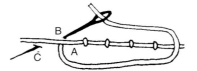

French knot

  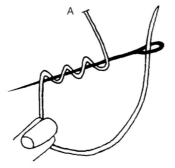 

Satin stitch

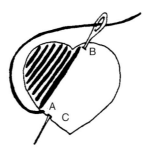

Long and short stitches

 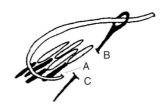

Incorporating small motifs within a decorative seam covering will create further visual interest.

Flowers, bees, and spiderweb with a spider incorporated into the seams; Black Vest, 1996.

Bird nest incorporated into a decorative seam covering; Black Vest, 1996.

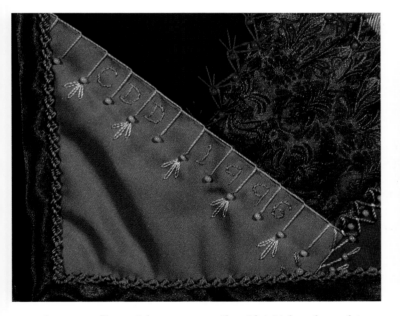

ABOVE AND RIGHT: *I document my quilts with initials and year date within a buttonhole stitch seam covering.*

Spiderweb with hanging spider; Multi-colored Vest, 1996.

Bullion stitch

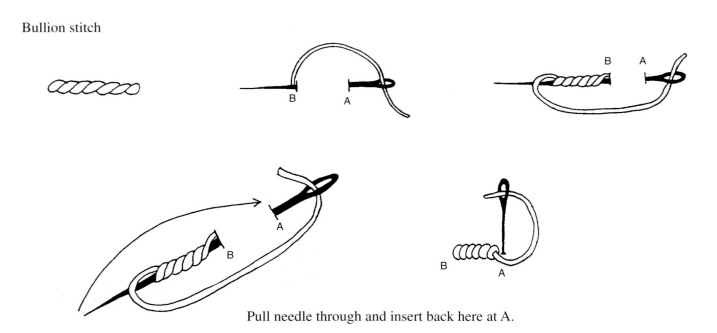

Pull needle through and insert back here at A.

FLOWERS

Bullion stitches   French knots   Lazy daisy stitches   Fly and straight stitches

Flowers and bees worked within a decorative seam covering

 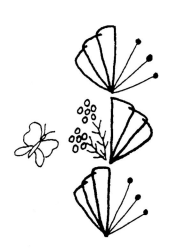

Flowers, bees, spiders, and spiderweb worked within a decorative seam covering

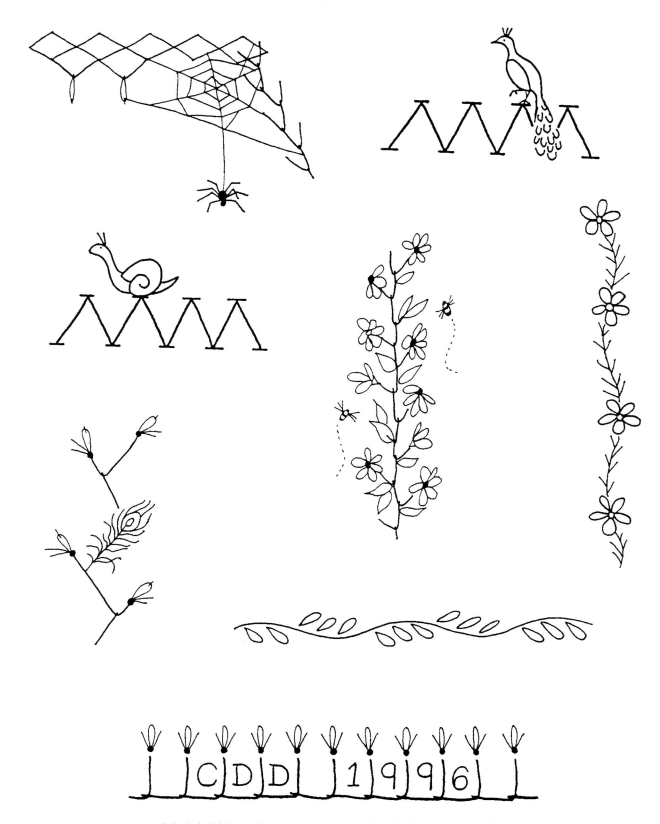

Stitch initials and date in a buttonhole-stitch seam covering

STITCH COMBINATIONS

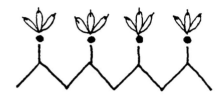

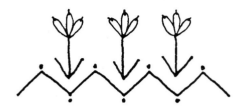

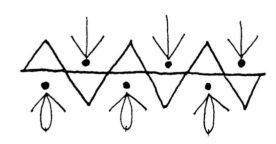

Woven straight stitch

Slanted buttonhole stitch

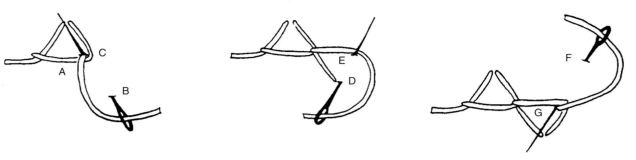

Slanted buttonhole stitch

Scroll stitch

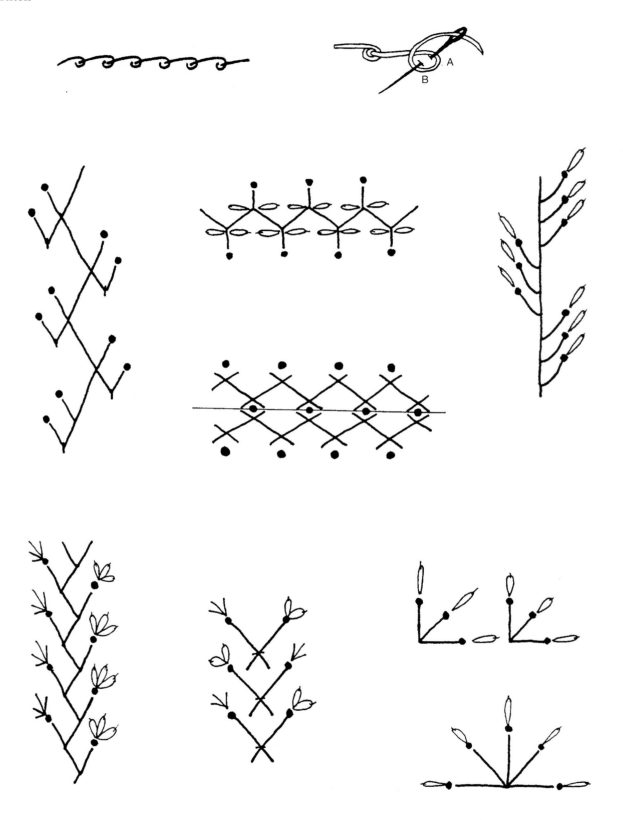

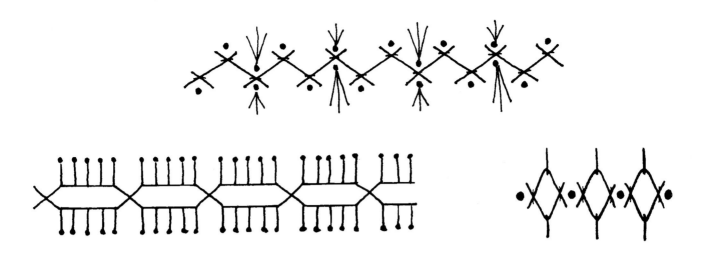

Woven herringbone stitch

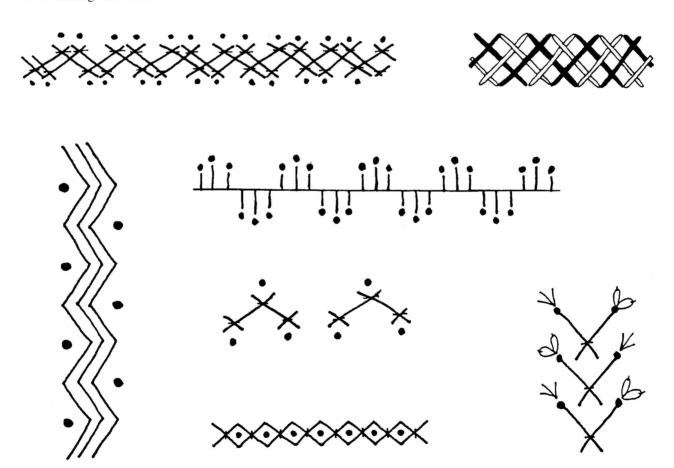

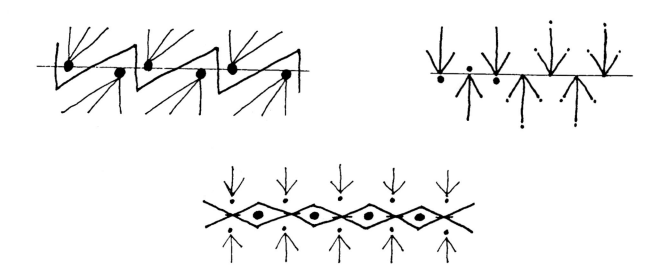

Straight stitch

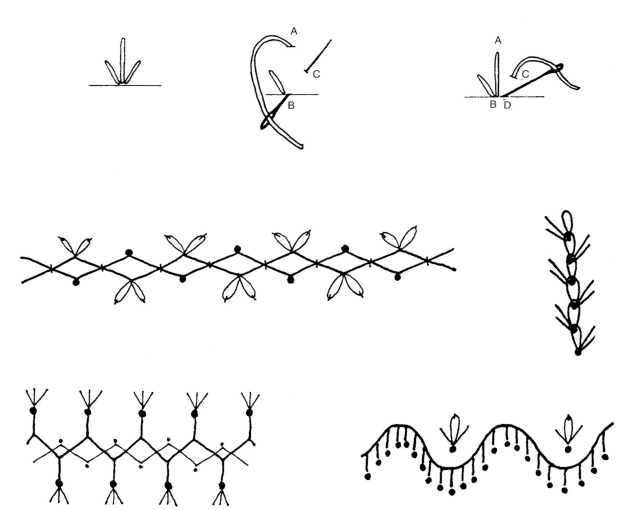

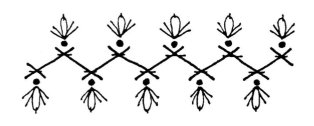
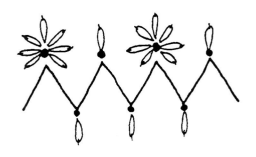

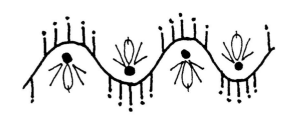
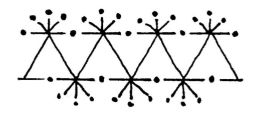

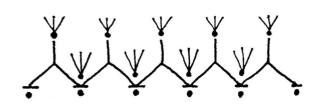
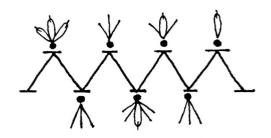

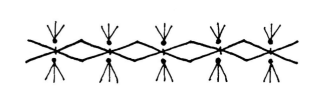
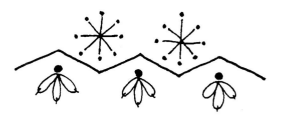

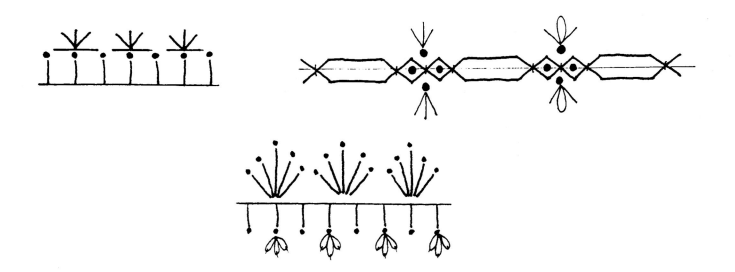

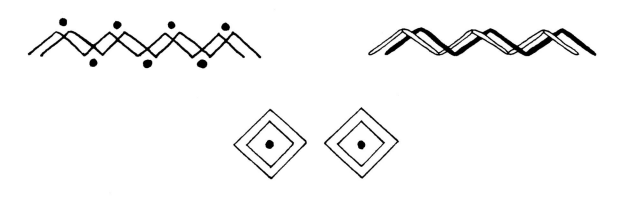

Woven straight stitch

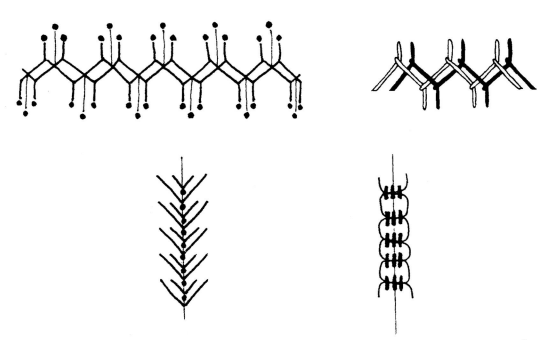

Woven cretan stitch

Double knot stitch

 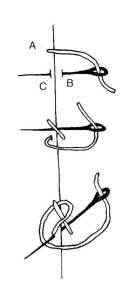 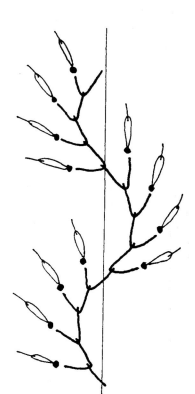 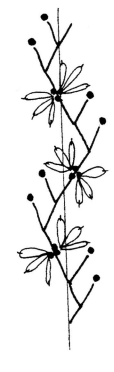

Twisted cretan stitch

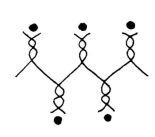 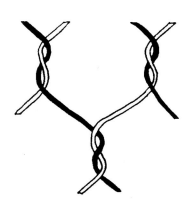

Corner

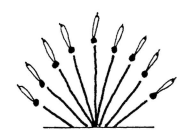 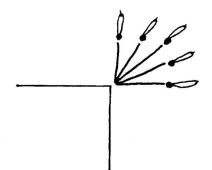 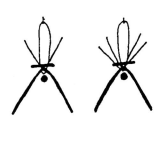

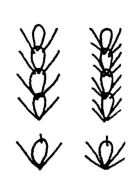
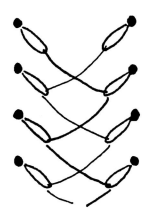

Open chain stitch

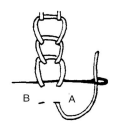

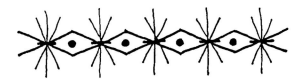

Woven thread

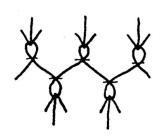

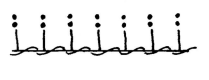

Up and down buttonhole stitch

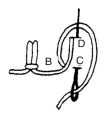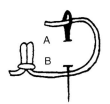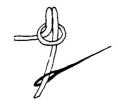

Woven straight stitch

Woven chain stitch

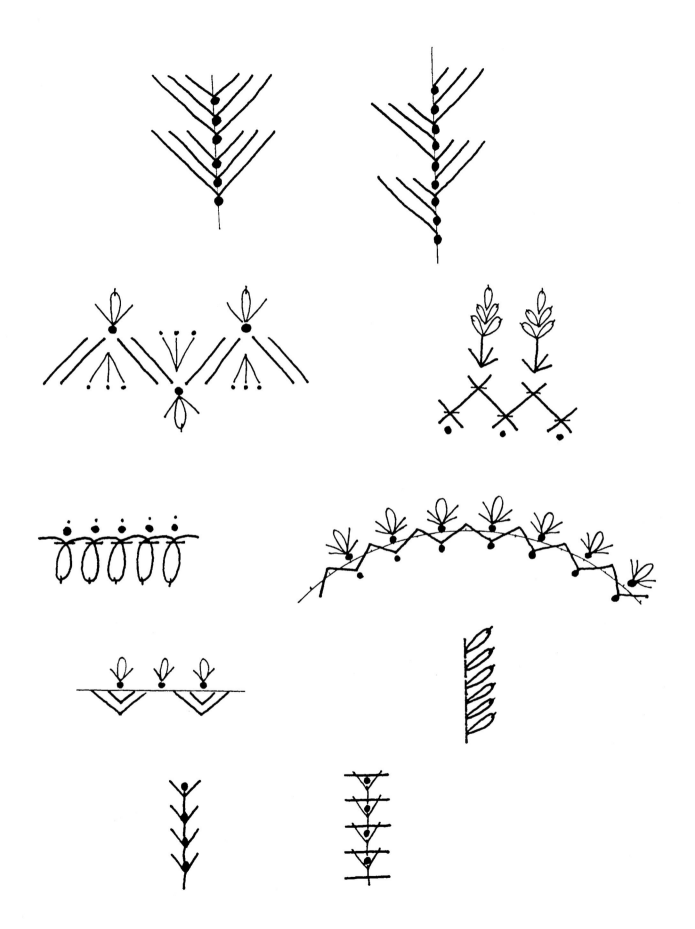

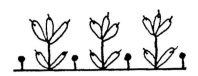

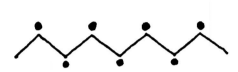

Knotted buttonhole stitch

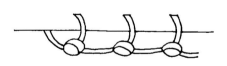

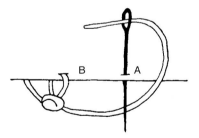

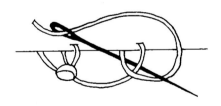

Beading

ACCENT BEADS add life and sparkle to crazy quilts. Glass seed beads can be found in hobby and craft shops, and petite beads are available at most needlepoint shops. A French knot will give a lovely effect as an alternative to beads.

Petite bead: size #14
Seed bead: size #11
Large bead: size #8 or #6
Beading thread: Nymo™ size 0 or 00, nylon monocord, or one strand cotton floss
Needle – Quilting Between: size 10 or smaller

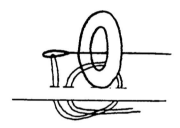

1. Double the thread in the needle and knot the ends together, keeping the finished length approximately 12 inches long.
2. To secure the bead in place, stitch through the bead once, then repeat to "lock" the bead in place.
3. At the border edge, bead only to the basted border line.
4. Bead one side of the decorative stitching, then cross the seam line and bead the opposite side. (See Figure 1.) Beading back and forth across the seam line may cause it to draw or pucker. (See Figure 2.)

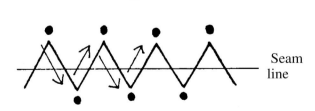

Figure 1.

Bead across one side, then bead the opposite side

Figure 2.

NO! Do not bead back and forth across the seam

Borders

CRAZY-QUILT borders are seen in a wide range of widths and styles, and may be lavishly embroidered, painted, or left plain.

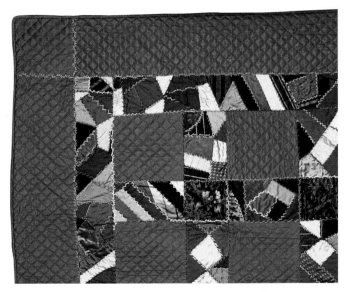

The 5 1/2-inch wide red satin border is a commercially manufactured machine-quilted coat lining fabric; the Contained Crazy Quilt, 1890.

Scallop and triangle border 3 1/2 to 4 inches wide; the Southwick Crazy Quilt, 1898.

An 8-inch velvet border; the Miller Crazy Quilt, 1890.

This 5-inch-wide border is comprised of 2-inch velvet and 3-inch satin panels; the Family Signature Crazy Quilt, 1995.

This 5-inch-wide velveteen border has painted flowers; the Carr Crazy Quilt, 1888.

This 2½-inch-wide border is from the Roosevelt Bears, a contained crazy quilt.

For one border panel:

1. Carefully trim away the excess foundation fabric from the quilt top, leaving approximately a ½- to 1-inch seam allowance.
2. Make a template the width of the border and the length of the poster board sheet from which the template is cut. If the border is to be 4 inches wide, the template should measure 4 inches wide.

```
┌─────────────────────────────────────┐
│                                      │
│            Template                  │   4″
│                                      │
└─────────────────────────────────────┘
```

3. Using the template, iron under both sides of the border fabric, then trim to a ½-inch seam allowance.
4. With the quilt top on a flat surface, measure both the width and diagonal for evenness. If the quilt top is not square, adjust by smoothing and stretching it slightly. (See Figure 1.)
5. Pin the side border panels using the basted border line as a guide. Next, pin the top and bottom border panels, overlapping the side borders and checking that the corners are square. (See Figure 1.)

Figure 1.

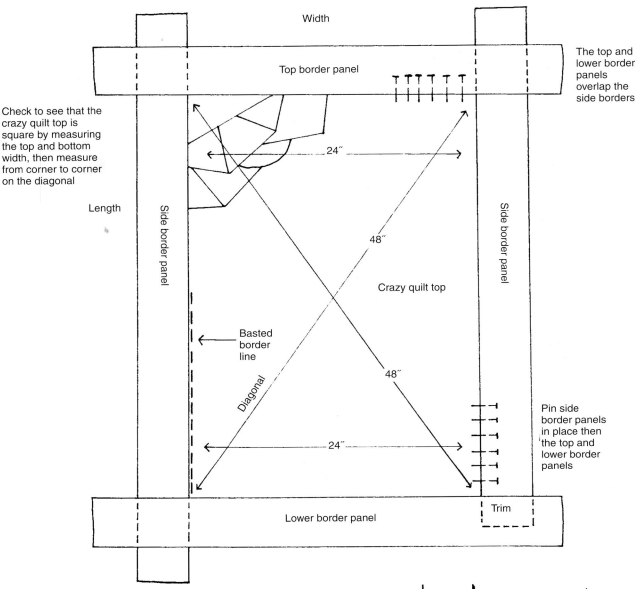

Width

Top border panel

The top and lower border panels overlap the side borders

Check to see that the crazy quilt top is square by measuring the top and bottom width, then measure from corner to corner on the diagonal

Length

Side border panel

24″

48″

Crazy quilt top

Side border panel

Basted border line

Diagonal

48″

Pin side border panels in place then the top and lower border panels

24″

Lower border panel

Trim

Note: The embroidery may have distorted the basted border line that is used as a guide in pinning the border in place. Be sure to keep the border panel straight when pinning in place.

6. Appliqué the borders in place. Cover this seam with a double knot stitch (see Stitches) working with a single strand of Kreinik Silk Serica™ or DMC pearl cotton #3 or #5.

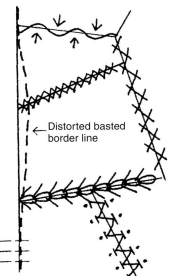

Border panel. Keep straight while pinning

Distorted basted border line

Double knot stitch on the inside border panel and knotted buttonhole stitch on the outside edge.

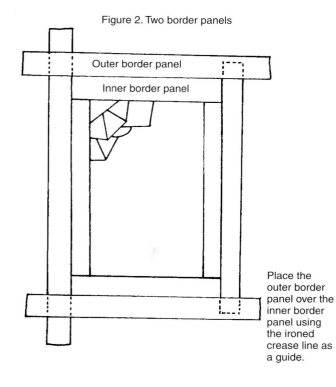

Figure 2. Two border panels

Outer border panel

Inner border panel

Place the outer border panel over the inner border panel using the ironed crease line as a guide.

Two border panels

1. Iron both sides of each border panel under. Using a border template, trim to a $1/2$-inch seam allowance.
2. Take the inner border panels and iron the outside edge seam allowance open. This will leave a crease line on the right side of the fabric.
3. Pin the folded-under side of the border panel to the quilt top.
4. Appliqué the inner border in place.
5. Using the crease line of the inner border as a placement guide, pin the outer border panel in place. Appliqué.

Batting

IN OLD CRAZY QUILTS batting was utilized in several ways. It was:

1. Placed between the crazy patches and foundation with the embroidery and decorative seam coverings stitched through the batting
2. Sandwiched between a foundation and quilt back fabric which could then be quilted
3. Layered between the crazy quilt top and back
4. Or not used at all.

Batting gives a crazy quilt a nice finished feel. Place a layer of batting between the crazy quilt top and backing fabric. The batting should extend an inch past the quilt top outside border edges. It will be trimmed later. I prefer Warm and Natural cotton batting in my quilts (see Resources).

Batting is placed between the patches and foundation and can be seen through the deteriorating silk, the Davis Crazy Quilt, 1892.

On the crazy-patch block sections batting is placed between the crazy patches and foundation. The black satin corner squares do not have any foundation, only brown batting; the Contained Crazy Quilt, circa 1890.

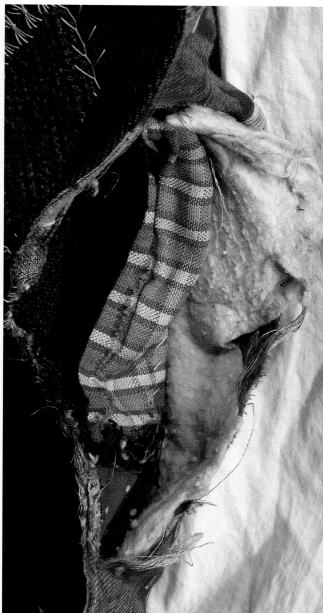

The quilted back has three layers: silk backing, batting, and foundation. From the quilt top, the quilted foundation back can be seen through a torn patch. From the back, the batting can be seen through the silk deterioration; the Southwick Crazy Quilt, 1892.

This quilt boasts thick cotton batting; the Snyder Crazy Quilt, 1899.

Backing

CHOOSE A FABRIC for the quilt back that will complement your quilt top. The fabric back should extend 2 inches past the outside border edges of the quilt top. Example: If the finished size (including borders) of the crazy quilt is 44 by 55 inches, the fabric back should measure 48 by 59 inches.

Securing the Layers

IN MANY old crazy quilts layers are secured together in the body of the quilt by tying or tacking. In quilts without a layer of batting, the top and back may be joined together only around the outside quilt edges. Traditional running-stitch quilting was rarely seen on crazy quilts because the layers and thickness of fabrics made it difficult to quilt through.

Layers of the Snyder Crazy Quilt, 1899, are tied with red yarn.

The Davis Crazy Quilt, 1892, originally was only a quilt top. It was backed with maroon velveteen and tied with wool in 1989.

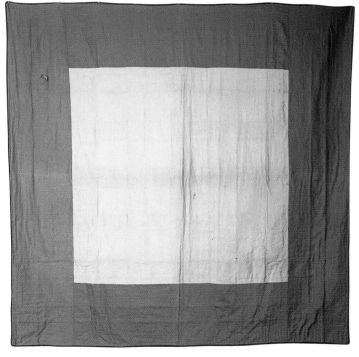

The Miller Crazy Quilt, 1890, is tacked.

The Contained Crazy Quilt, 1890, does not have any batting. The top and back are tacked together by random stitches hidden in the seams.

1. Place the fabric back, batting, and quilt top together in that order, smoothing all layers. Be sure the fabric back extends 2 inches around the outside border edge of the quilt top.
2. Use a yardstick and chalk pencil to measure and mark evenly spaced increments on the quilt top. As you mark the row, pin the layers together just above each mark. Depending on the size of the quilt, increments should be between 4 and 6 inches apart. (See Figure 1.)

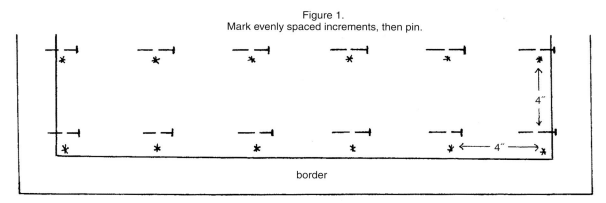

Figure 1.
Mark evenly spaced increments, then pin.

border

4″

Mark evenly spaced increments, then pin.

Tying

1. To determine the length of thread you will need to tie each row, count the number of chalk marks in the row, and multiply by 8 inches. Example: If you have five tie chalk marks, you will need 40 inches of thread (5 marks x 8 inches = 40 inches). Thread your needle with Kreinik Silk Serica™ or DMC pearl cotton #3 or #5, and do not knot the end.
2. Place the quilt on a flat surface and, starting at the first row, insert the needle from the back at point A. Making a $^1/8$- to $^1/4$-inch stitch on the quilt top, insert the needle at point B to the back. (See Figure 1.)

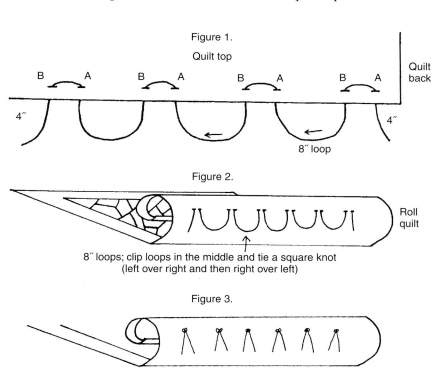

Figure 1.

Quilt top

Quilt back

4″

4″

8″ loop

Figure 2.

Roll quilt

8″ loops; clip loops in the middle and tie a square knot
(left over right and then right over left)

Figure 3.

Tie square knots and trim ends evenly

Square knot

3. Stitch across the entire row, making a stitch at each chalk mark. Leave a loop on the back approximately 8 inches long between each stitch. (See Figure 1.)
4. Roll the quilt until the row of loops on the back can be seen. Clip each loop in the middle, leaving two 4-inch tails for each tie. (See Figure 2.)
5. Tie a square knot and evenly trim the tails along the row. Leave the tails $1^1/2$ to 2 inches long. (See Figure 3.)
6. Continue to roll the quilt, one row at a time, until all rows are tied.

Note: For a heavier knot, double the thread in the needle.

Note: To tie one knot at a time, cut a single 8-inch thread length and insert from the back at point A. Make a $^1/8$- to $^1/4$-inch stitch and insert at point B. Tie a square knot at the back and trim the ends. (See Figure 4.)

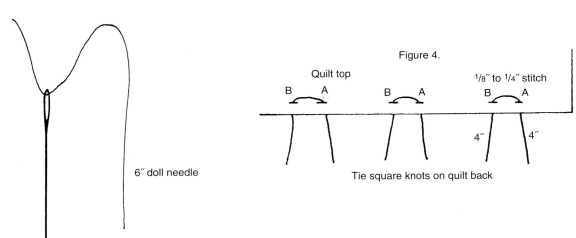

Figure 4.

Quilt top

B   A   B   A   ⅛″ to ¼″ stitch

                               B   A

6″ doll needle

4″   4″

Tie square knots on quilt back

Tacking

1. Mark even increments on the quilt top and pin. (See Tying section, Figure 1.) Cut a length of thread one and one-half times the width of the row. Thread a 6-inch doll needle and knot the end.
2. Insert the doll needle on the first row between the quilt top and batting layer, inserting the needle up through the quilt top at chalk-mark point A. (See Figure 1.)
3. Make a ⅛- to ¼-inch backstitch, inserting the needle down through all layers to the back at point B. (See Figure 2.)
4. Bring the needle back up through all layers at point A again. Make another backstitch, inserting the needle at point B and sliding it between the quilt top and batting. Continue to the next chalk tack mark. Firmly secure each completed tack stitch. (See Figure 3.)
5. Tack each row individually. Knot the thread end inside the quilt's border edges.
6. Continue rolling the quilt and tack each row.

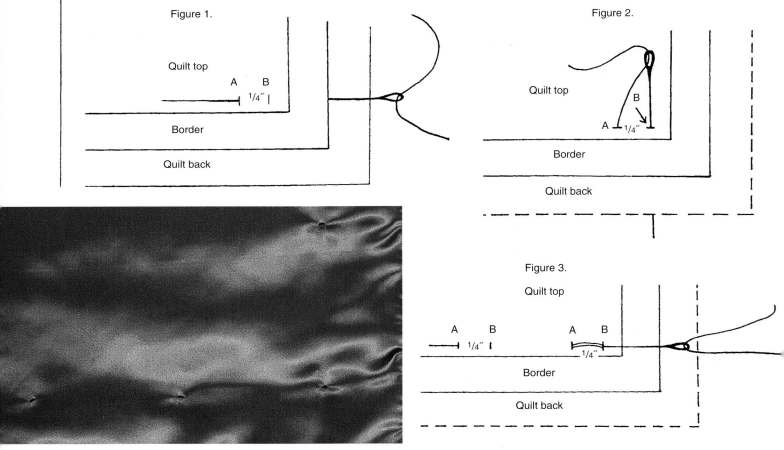

Figure 1.

Quilt top

A   B
        ¼″

Border

Quilt back

Figure 2.

Quilt top

B

A   ¼″

Border

Quilt back

Figure 3.

Quilt top

A   B   A   B
    ¼″   ¼″

Border

Quilt back

Tacking on a miniature crazy quilt back.

Finishing the Border Edges

1. Carefully trim the batting to the quilt top border edges.
2. Fold the quilt's fabric back to the inside, matching it to the top border edge, and then finger press. (See Figure 1.) Fold the border panel ends on the quilt top to the inside. (See Figure 2.)
3. Pin all border edges together. (See Figure 3.)
4. Stitch the quilt edges together using Kreinik Silk Serica™, or DMC pearl cotton #3 or #5, and a double knot buttonhole stitch. (See Stitches.)
5. Many crazy quilt edges are finished with a seam binding. Match all the quilt layer edges, pin the seam binding in place, and stitch.

Figure 1.

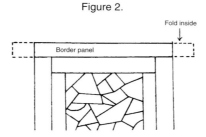

Figure 2.

Figure 3.

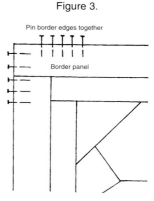

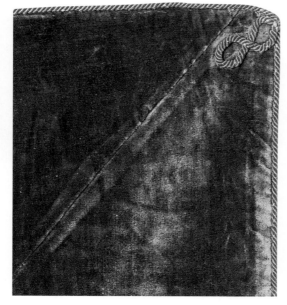

Finished knotted buttonhole stitch on a border edge.

RIGHT: *The quilt edges are hand stitched together and then embellished with a maroon cord. At the corners, the cord is hand stitched into a figure eight; the Miller Crazy Quilt, 1890.*

Red satin seam binding hand stitched in place; the Contained Crazy Quilt, 1890.

The silk seam binding is hand stitched around the scalloped border; the Southwick Crazy Quilt, 1898.

A Final Touch

TO DISPLAY the quilt as a wall hanging, appliqué a sleeve onto the back of the quilt. With a piece of quilt backing fabric, make a 4-inch-wide border panel that extends the width of the finished quilt. Fold the panel ends under ($^1/_2$ inch) and appliqué the sleeve in place across the quilt's top back so that a hanging rod may be slipped through it.

Document the quilt with a label stitched onto the back. Always include on the label: who made the quilt, the date it was completed, its size, and who the quilt is for. You also may wish to photograph the quilt and keep a journal with detailed information about the making of the crazy quilt. This documentation should accompany the quilt in the future.

My first crazy quilt made for my youngest daughter, Jennifer, 1993, 52″ x 62″.

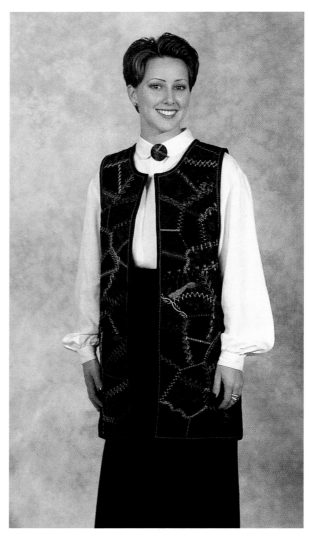

Black on Black Crazy Patch Vest modeled by my eldest daughter, Frances, 1995.

Miniature Crazy Quilt, 1994, 15″ x 18″. This small quilt won first place in Miniature Quilts *magazine's 1994 Miniatures from the Heart Contest, Other Techniques Category.*

Tips For Crazy Quilt Care

Because crazy quilts are made from many different fabrics and embellishments, careful handling should be exercised to protect and preserve them. Never wash the crazy quilt because water may cause the fabrics or threads to spot, bleed, or possibly shrink. Also avoid dry cleaning because this may cause the fabrics to dry out. Gentle vacuuming is the safest way to surface clean an embellished crazy quilt. To protect the quilt top while vacuuming, place clean window screening or bridal netting over the area to be vacuumed.

When storing a folded quilt, wrap it in acid-free paper or unbleached muslin, padding the folds to prevent creasing. Never store a quilt in plastic! Take the quilt out and refold it several times a year. An alternative to folding is rolling the quilt in muslin. Roll the quilt carefully and not too tightly, with the embroidered patches facing the outside. This will help to avoid creasing and wrinkling the embroidered patches.

Place strips of cedar wood near the stored quilt to help deter insects, such as moths, from snacking. Mothballs may damage the quilt fabrics, so avoid using them.

Store the quilt in a clean, dry, and dark place.

When displaying the quilt, avoid exposing it to direct sunlight, fluorescent lights, or bright household lights for any length of time. These lights could cause fabric deterioration and fading.

Above all, enjoy and appreciate these unique and special works of needle art.

Oriental-theme crazy quilt, 1994, 50˝ x 55˝. The embroidered motifs were inspired by Traditional Chinese Designs *and* Needlework Dragons *and* Other Mythical Creatures. *(See Resources.)*

Black on Black Crazy Quilt, 1995, 50″ x 55″. This quilt won first place for Crazy Quilts at the 1995 International Quilt Association's annual quilt show. It is entirely stitched by hand, as are all my quilts.

Family Signature Crazy Quilt, 1995, 47″ x 52″. This quilt garnered a first-place award at the 1995 Marin Quilt & Needle Arts Show and was exhibited at Quilt Expo V, held in Lyon, France, in 1996.

Hearts and Flowers, 1996, 44˝ x 54˝. The border and many motifs on this quilt were adapted from The Embroiderer's Country Album *and* The Embroiderer's Countryside *by English embroidery artist Helen Stevens (see Resources). The flower bouquet and other motifs were featured in the magazine* Inspirations, *Issue No. 6, 1995 (see Resources). This quilt won first place and Viewers Choice awards at the 1996 Marin Quilt & Needle Arts Show and the 1998 Road to California quilt show. It also received a first place award for crazy quilts at the 1996 International Quilt Association quilt show.*

The Roosevelt Bears, a contained crazy quilt, 1998, 45″ x 57″. The embroidered patches on this story quilt were adapted from the children's books The Roosevelt Bears: Their Travels and Adventures *and* The Roosevelt Bears Go to Washington, *by Seymour Eaton (see Resources). My grandfather, Wilson Carter, read these stories to me as a child. This quilt received a second place award at the 1998 International Quilt Association quilt show in the mixed media category (formerly the crazy quilt category).*

Part 111

How to Make an American Quilt

Patterns for the Crazy Patch Heart Block and the Movie Crazy Quilt

Crazy Patch Heart Block from the wedding quilt Where Love Resides.

Crazy Patch Heart Block

THIS CRAZY PATCH Heart Block is one of sixteen blocks that make up Finn's wedding quilt, Where Love Resides, as seen in the 1995 Universal City Studios, Inc. and Amblin Entertainment, Inc. film *How to Make an American Quilt*. The finished block measures 15 by 15 inches. When assembling the heart block, refer to the basic crazy-quilt instructions.

1. Cut the templates from poster board.
2. On 1 square yard of foundation fabric outline a block measuring 15 by 15 inches.
3. Using the border templates as a guide, outline the heart in the middle of the block, being sure to draw both the inside and outside border edges.
4. Pin the crazy patches in place, using the inside heart border outline as a guide. Follow the template numbers for correct patch placement. (See Figure 2.)
5. Trim seam allowances, then appliqué the patches in place.
6. Transfer the Eiffel Tower onto the center of patch 1, then outline using the couch stitch. Suggested thread for stitching the Eiffel Tower is Kreinik fine #8 braid #10HL.
7. Cover the seams with decorative stitches, following the stitch pattern guide. Accent seam coverings with beads or French knots. (See Figure 1.)
8. Iron a seam allowance on both sides of the border fabric, using the border template as a guide. Trim seam allowances.
9. Following the outside border outline, ease the border into place, then pin and appliqué.

The heart block may be finished into a pillow or wall hanging, or it can be incorporated into a larger quilt. See Resources for information on obtaining the remaining pattern for Where Love Resides.

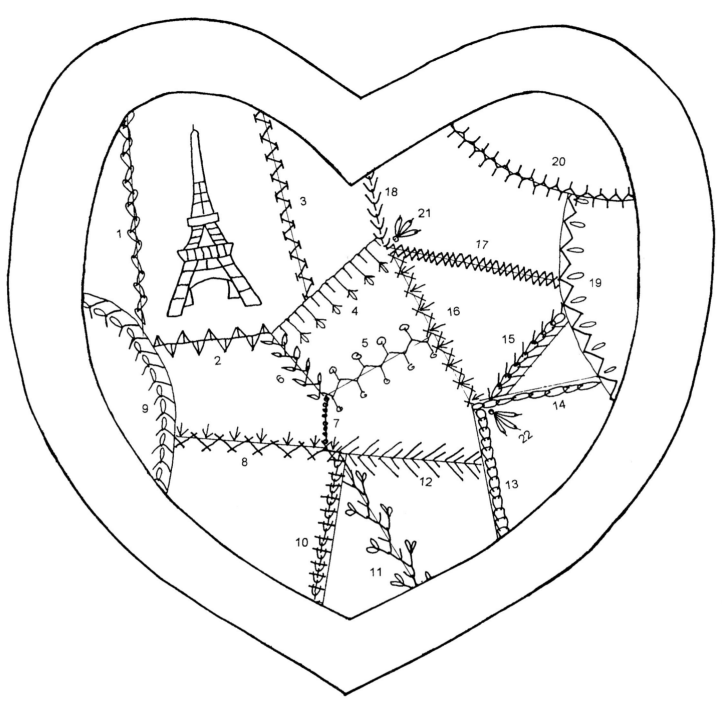

Stitches are shown smaller than actual size.

1. Chain stitch
2. Slanted buttonhole stitch
3. Chevron stitch
4. Buttonhole stitch, lazy daisy stitch, straight stitch
5. Cretan stitch, French knot
6. Lazy daisy stitch, straight stitch
7. Double knot stitch
8. Herringbone stitch, straight stitch
9. Lazy daisy stitch, straight stitch
10. Fly stitch, straight stitch

11. Feather and lazy daisy stitches
12. Straight stitch
13. Open chain stitch
14. Closed chain stitch
15. Chain stitch, straight stitch
16. Herringbone stitch, straight stitch
17. Straight stitch
18. Fly stitch
19. Straight stitch, lazy daisy stitch
20. Cretan stitch
21. Lazy daisy stitch
22. Lazy daisy stitch

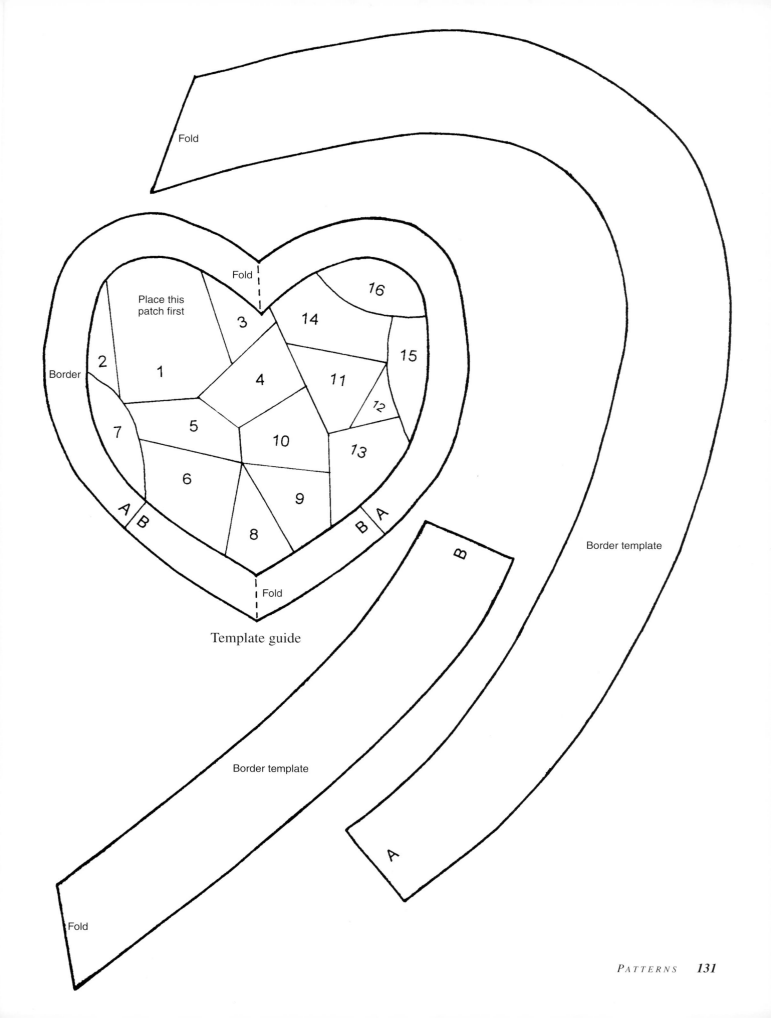

Fold

Fold

Place this
patch first

Border

Template guide

Border template

Border template

Fold

Fold

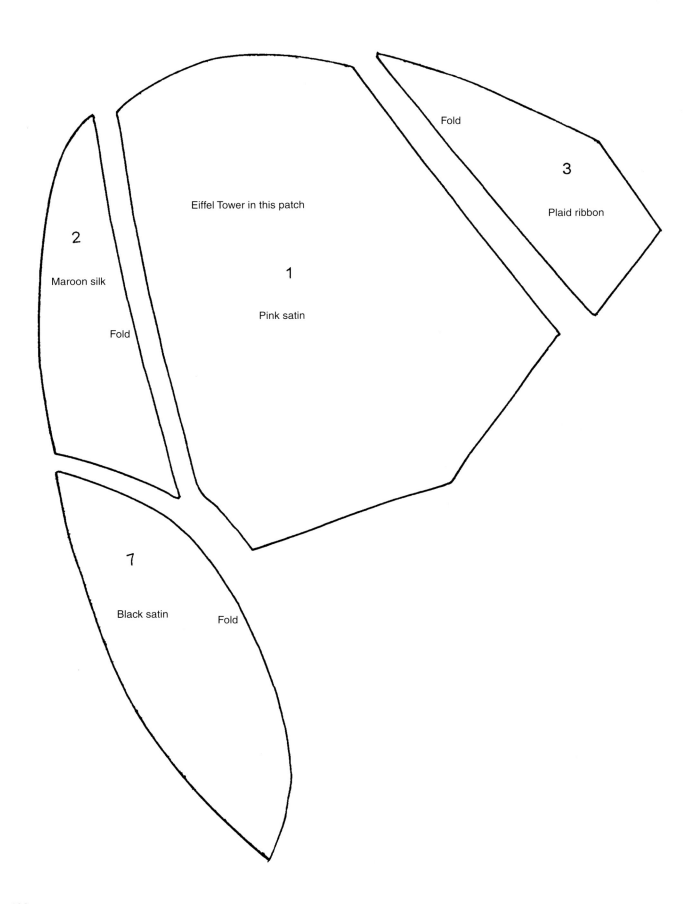

Eiffel Tower in this patch

2

Maroon silk

Fold

1

Pink satin

Fold

3

Plaid ribbon

7

Black satin

Fold

The full-size templates are numbered in order of placement with suggested fabrics.

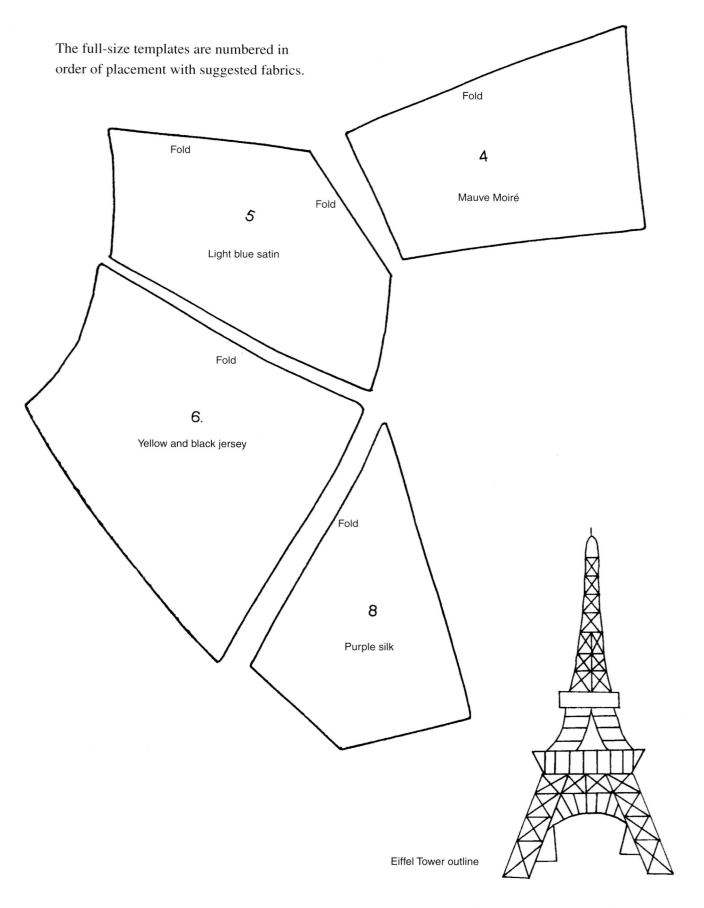

Fold

4

Mauve Moiré

Fold

Fold

5

Light blue satin

Fold

6.

Yellow and black jersey

Fold

8

Purple silk

Eiffel Tower outline

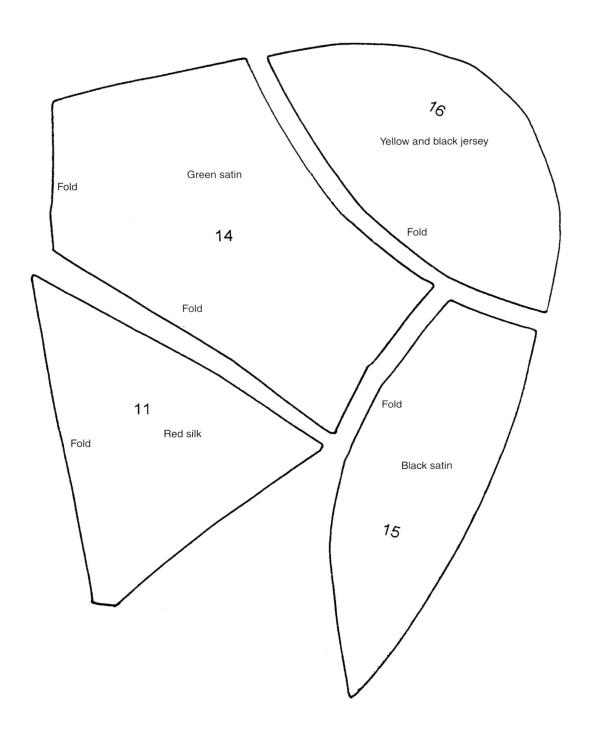

Green satin

Fold

14

Fold

16

Yellow and black jersey

Fold

Fold

11

Fold

Red silk

Fold

Black satin

15

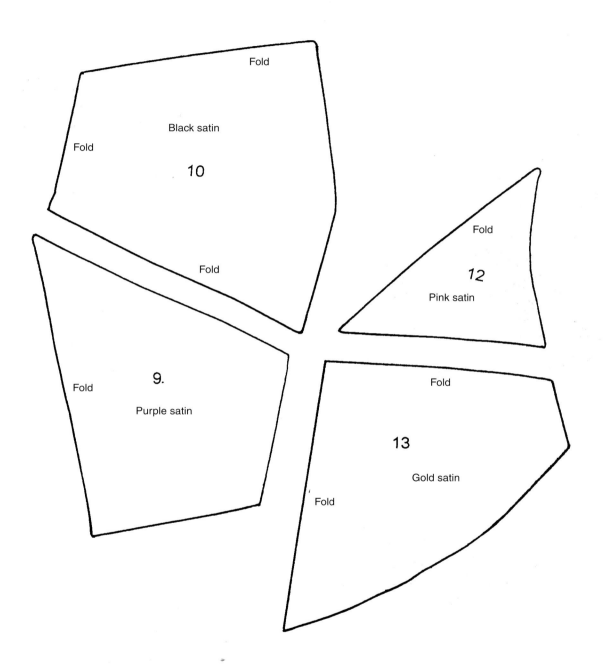

Fold

Black satin

Fold

10

Fold

Fold

9.

Purple satin

Fold

Fold

12

Pink satin

Fold

13

Gold satin

Fold

The Movie Crazy Quilt

This aged stone-washed crazy quilt was created for the film
How to Make an American Quilt; *the Movie Crazy Quilt,*
1994, 32¹/₂ ˝ x 54˝.

THIS 32¹/₂-by-54-inch crib-size crazy-quilt top was created for the 1995 film *How to Make an American Quilt.* The quilt was seen briefly in an opening scene, draped over Finn's lap as she sat on the floor. The studio requested that I design and stitch two identical crazy-quilt tops within sixty days. Both tops were stitched with DMC pearl cotton and DMC cotton floss accented with French knots. The quilt seen in the film was aged and stone-washed; the other quilt remained untouched as a standby.

After filming was completed, I was asked to finish backing the standby quilt, which was then presented to Winona Ryder, who starred in the role of Finn. I acquired the aged stone-washed quilt for my collection. Later, I duplicated the Movie Crazy Quilt several times, stitching it with silk thread and embellishing it with beads.

Refer to the basic instructions to complete the quilt. For fabric suggestions, refer to the numbered template fabric list and photographs as a guide. For the decorative seam coverings, select thread colors that will complement or contrast with the fabric patches.

1. Using templates, piece the quilt top on a foundation fabric. The numbered templates do not correspond to the order of patch placement; they only show patch location on the quilt top. Piece in the order easiest for you. (See Figure 1.)
2. Appliqué the patches in place.
3. Transfer and embroider motifs.
4. Following the stitching guide, stitch the decorative seam coverings.
5. Add beads or French knots to the decorative seam coverings.
6. Attach borders. The inside border panel measures 2 inches and is navy blue velvet; the outside border panel measures 3 inches and is black satin.
7. Back the quilt with black satin, then tie or tack.
8. Finish with a label and hanging sleeve on the quilt back.

This quilt is stitched with silk threads, then beaded; the Movie Crazy Quilt, 1996, 32¹/₂″ x 54″.

Details of sections.

Details of sections.

Details of sections.

Numbered Template Patch Guide and Fabric List

Suggested fabrics

1: Striped aqua satin
*2, 16, 65: Cotton print
3: Cream satin
*4, 71: Navy blue taffeta
*5, 70: Maroon moiré
*6, 58, 73: Striped ribbon
*7, 60: Gold satin
*8, 10, 18, 24, 31A, 36, 38,
   37, 41, 43, 59, 68: Ribbons
   with floral design
9: Dark green velvet
*11, 64: Orange satin
12: Moss green plaid taffeta
*13, 52: Moss green satin
14: Soft pink velveteen
15: Mauve cotton
*17, 79: Pink satin
*19, 33, 57, 3-inch border:
   Black satin
20: Maroon silk
*21, 77: Beige satin
22: Cotton brocade
23: Seafoam moiré
*25, 53: Baby blue satin
26: Aqua silk
27: Striped silk
28: Rust satin
29: Navy silk
30: Dark gold velvet
31: Apricot moiré
32: Green polished cotton
34: Aqua velveteen
*35, 61, 2-inch border:
   Navy blue velvet
39: Baby blue moiré
40: Blue/red plaid cotton
42: Aqua silk
*44, 55: Red silk
45: Pink moiré
46: Dark blue taffeta
47: Medium gold satin
48: Pink satin
49: Brown satin
50: Maroon silk
51: Black/silver silk
54: Leaf green velveteen
56: Pale green moiré
62: Medium blue taffeta
63: Turquoise cotton
66: Purple velveteen
67: Purple satin
69: Blue/gray silk
72: Sky blue satin
74: Medium green satin
75: Maroon cotton
76: Orange satin
78: Cotton with animal design
80: Navy cotton

* Denotes the same fabric on
   these patches

THE MOVIE CRAZY QUILT

Full-size templates with embroidery
motifs and suggested fabrics.

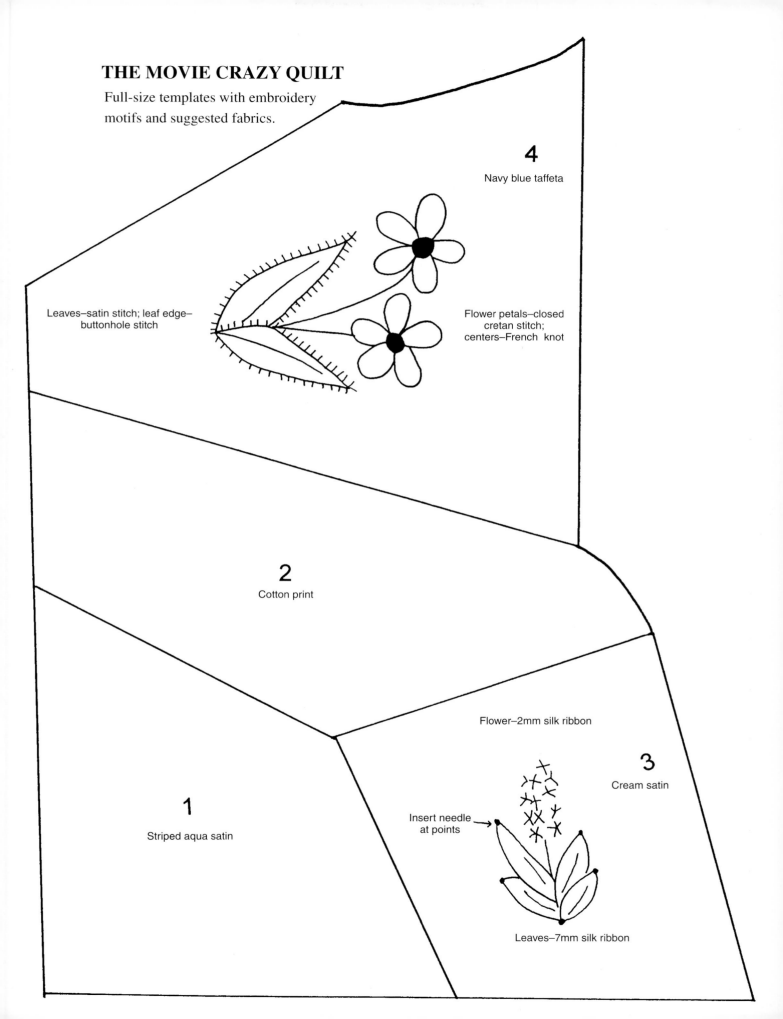

4

Navy blue taffeta

Leaves–satin stitch; leaf edge–
buttonhole stitch

Flower petals–closed
cretan stitch;
centers–French knot

2

Cotton print

Flower–2mm silk ribbon

3

Cream satin

1

Striped aqua satin

Insert needle
at points →

Leaves–7mm silk ribbon

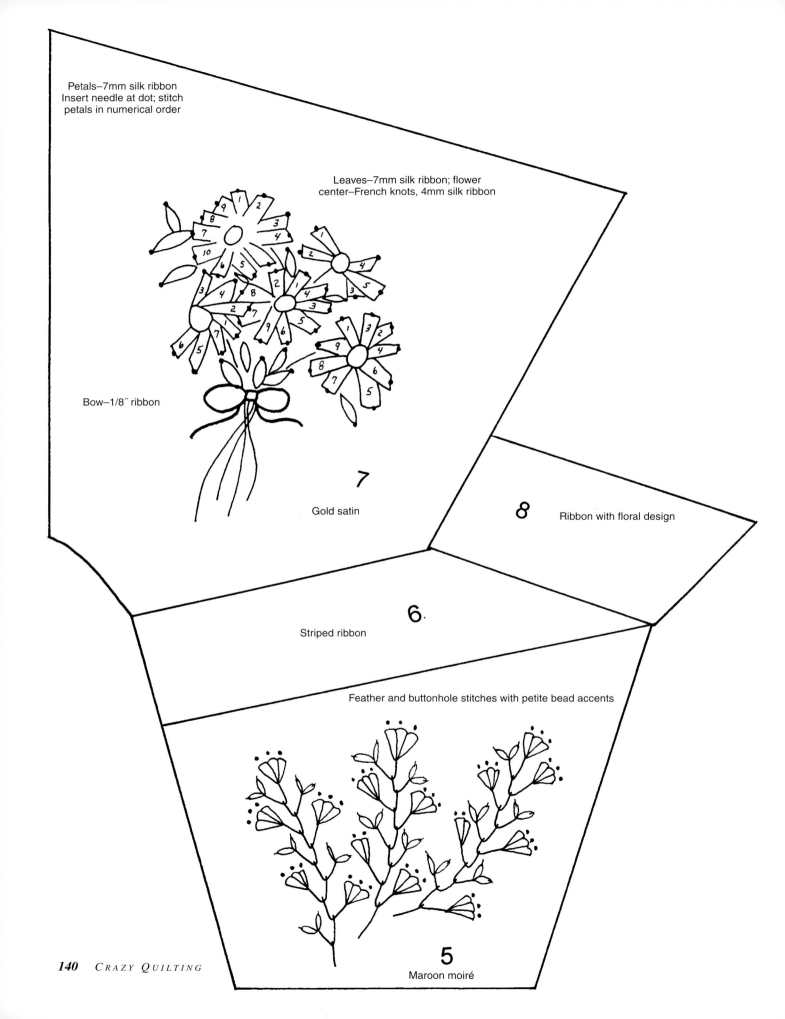

Petals–7mm silk ribbon
Insert needle at dot; stitch
petals in numerical order

Leaves–7mm silk ribbon; flower
center–French knots, 4mm silk ribbon

Bow–1/8″ ribbon

7

Gold satin

8   Ribbon with floral design

6.

Striped ribbon

Feather and buttonhole stitches with petite bead accents

5
Maroon moiré

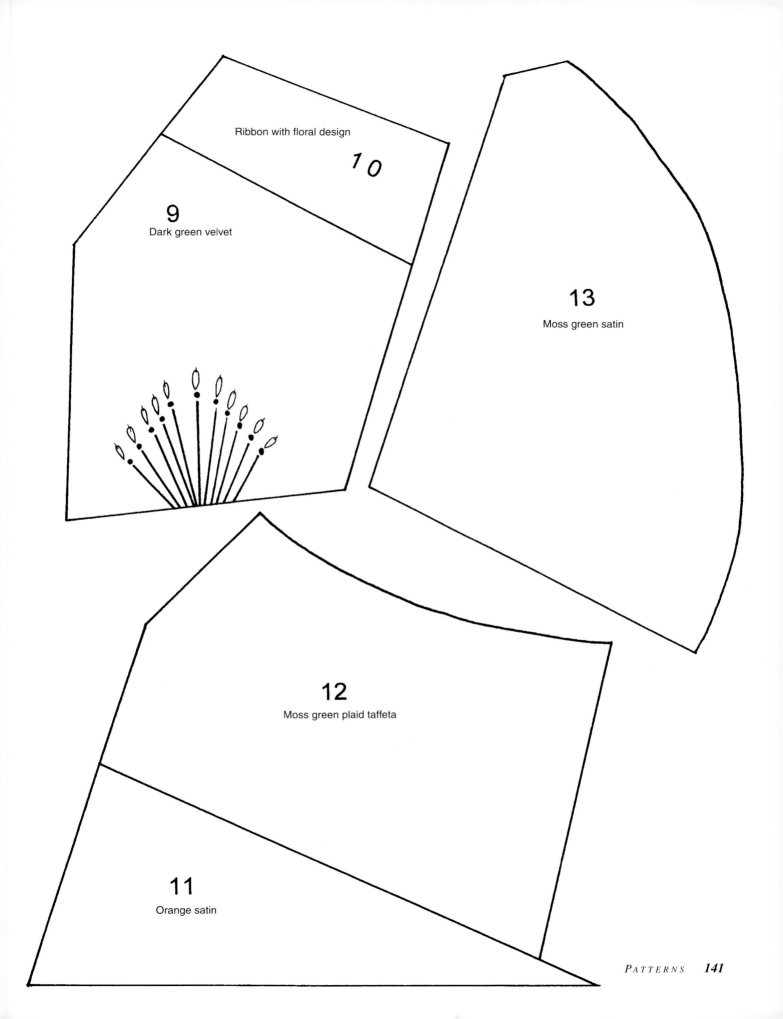

Ribbon with floral design

1 0

9

Dark green velvet

13

Moss green satin

12

Moss green plaid taffeta

11

Orange satin

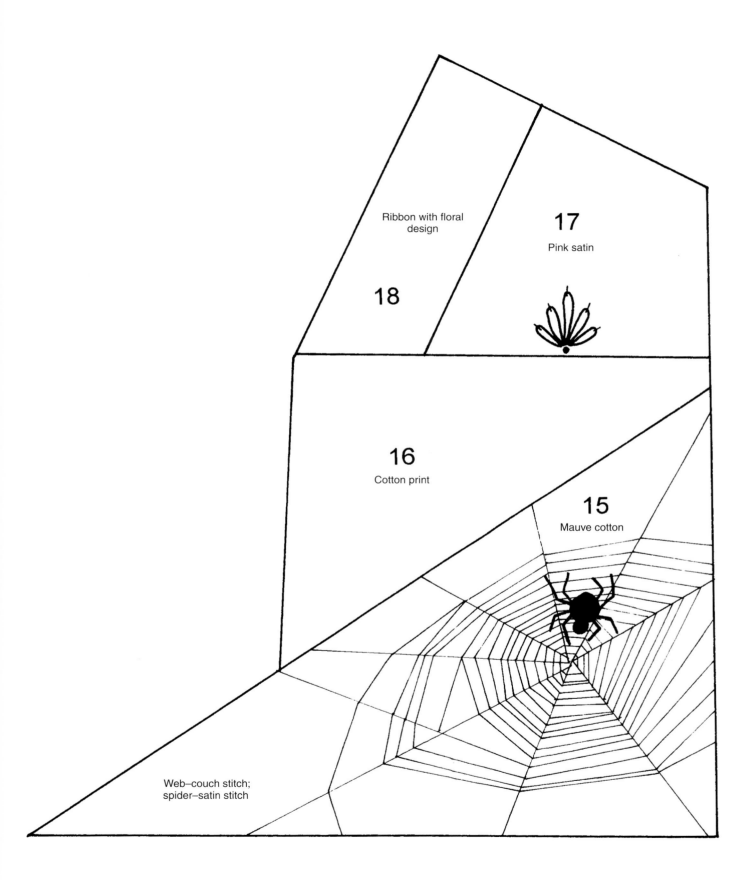

Ribbon with floral design

18

17

Pink satin

16

Cotton print

15

Mauve cotton

Web–couch stitch;
spider–satin stitch

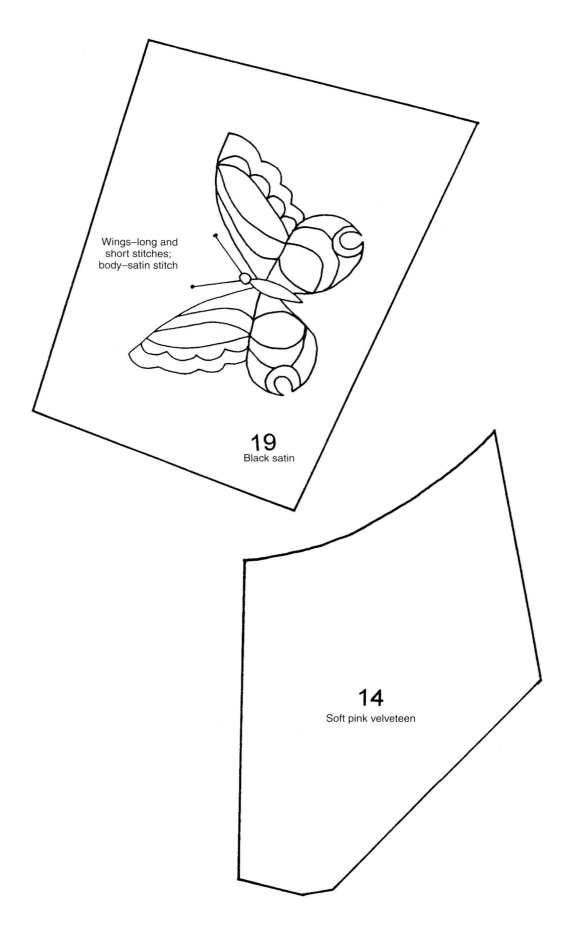

Wings–long and
short stitches;
body–satin stitch

19
Black satin

14
Soft pink velveteen

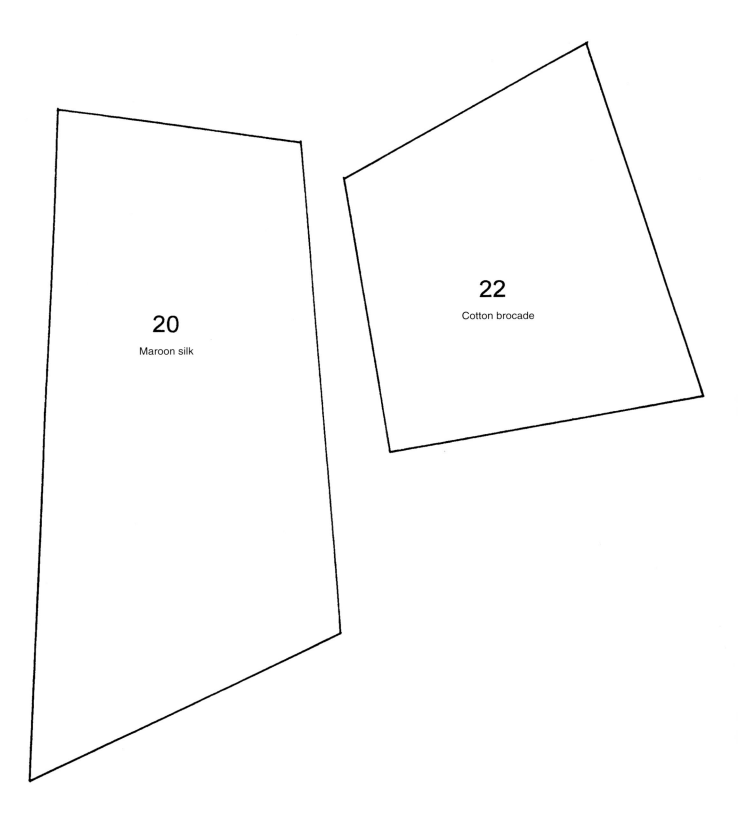

20

Maroon silk

22

Cotton brocade

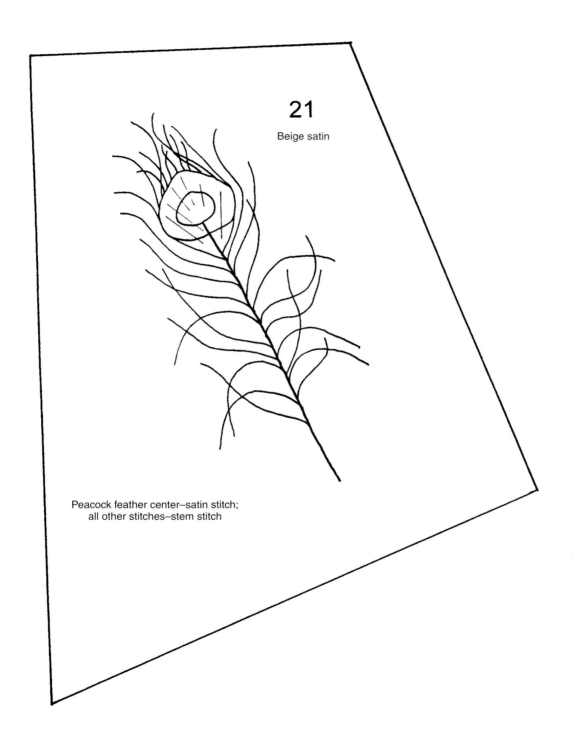

21

Beige satin

Peacock feather center–satin stitch;
all other stitches–stem stitch

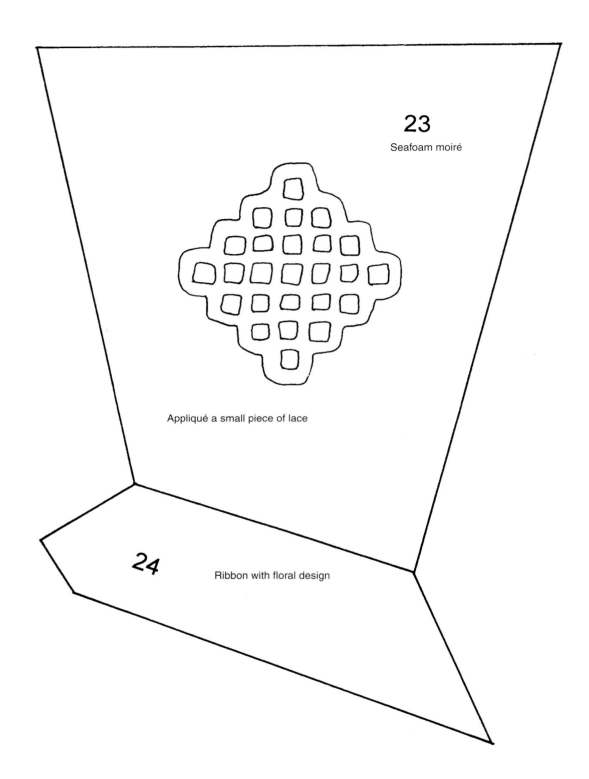

23

Seafoam moiré

Appliqué a small piece of lace

24   Ribbon with floral design

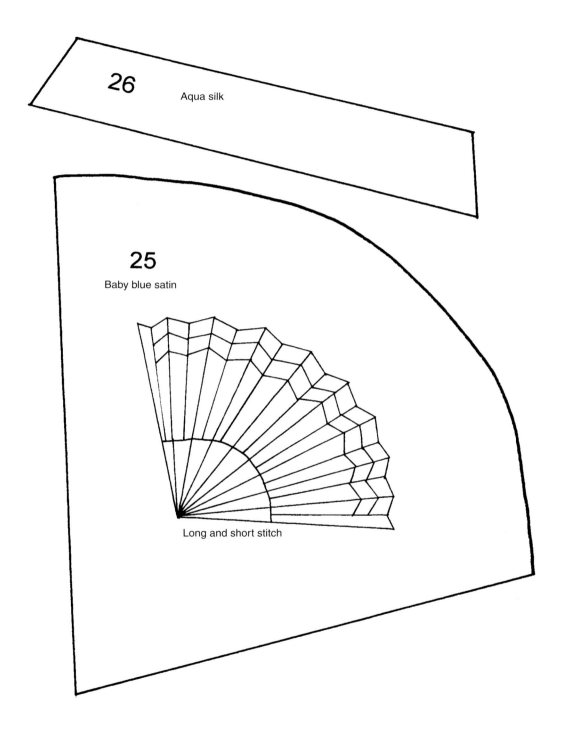

26

Aqua silk

25

Baby blue satin

Long and short stitch

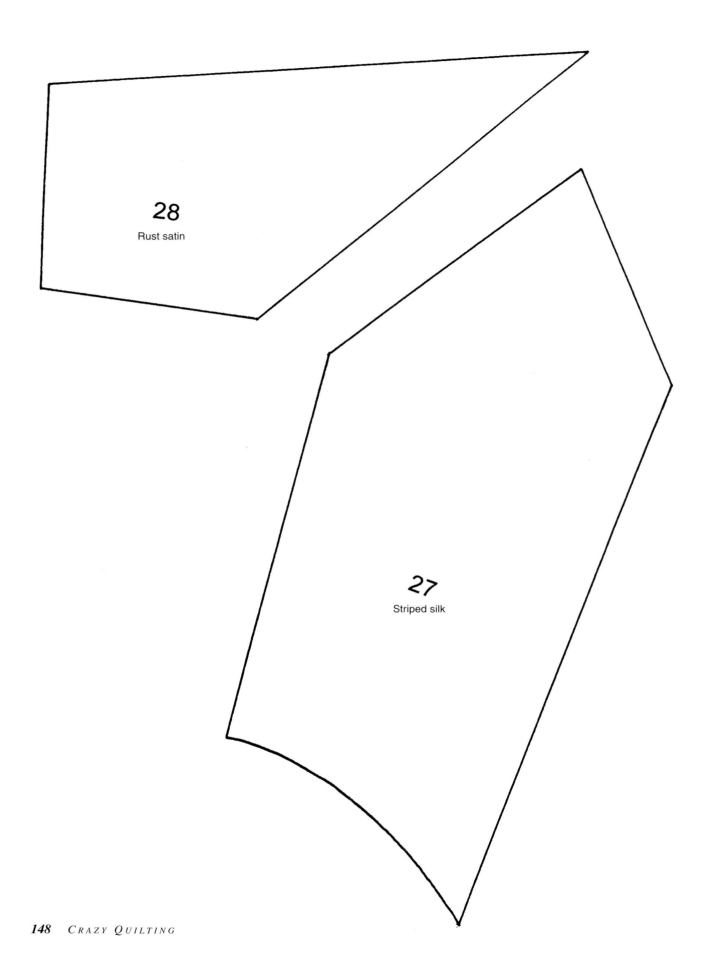

28
Rust satin

27
Striped silk

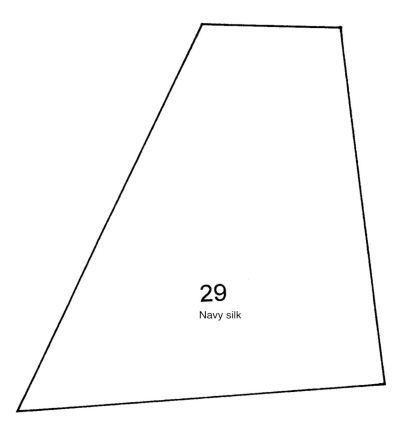

29

Navy silk

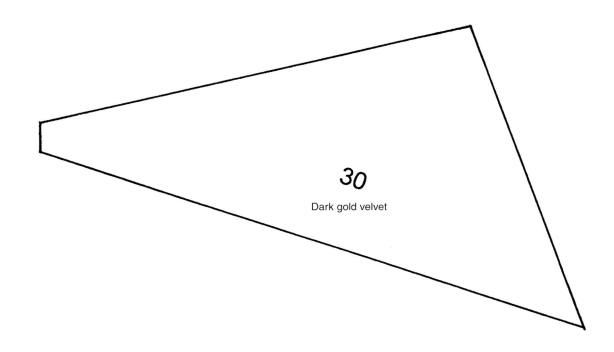

30

Dark gold velvet

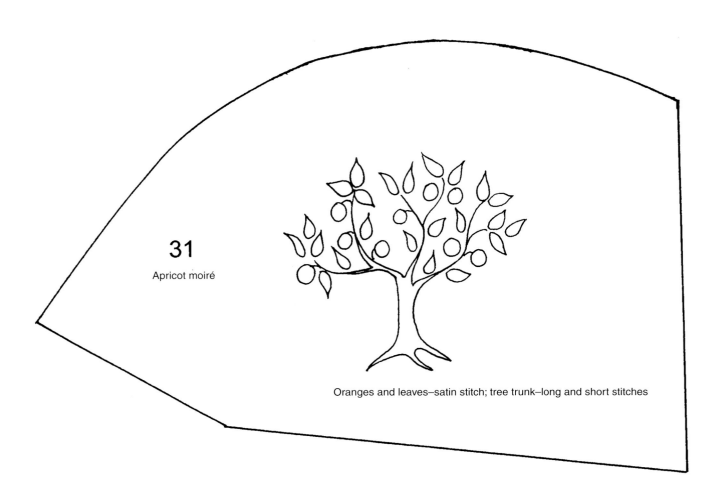

31

Apricot moiré

Oranges and leaves—satin stitch; tree trunk—long and short stitches

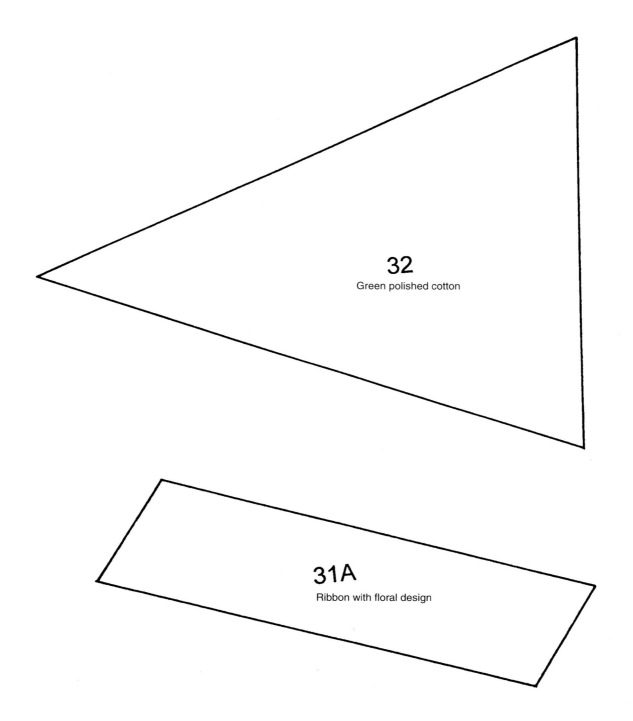

32
Green polished cotton

31A
Ribbon with floral design

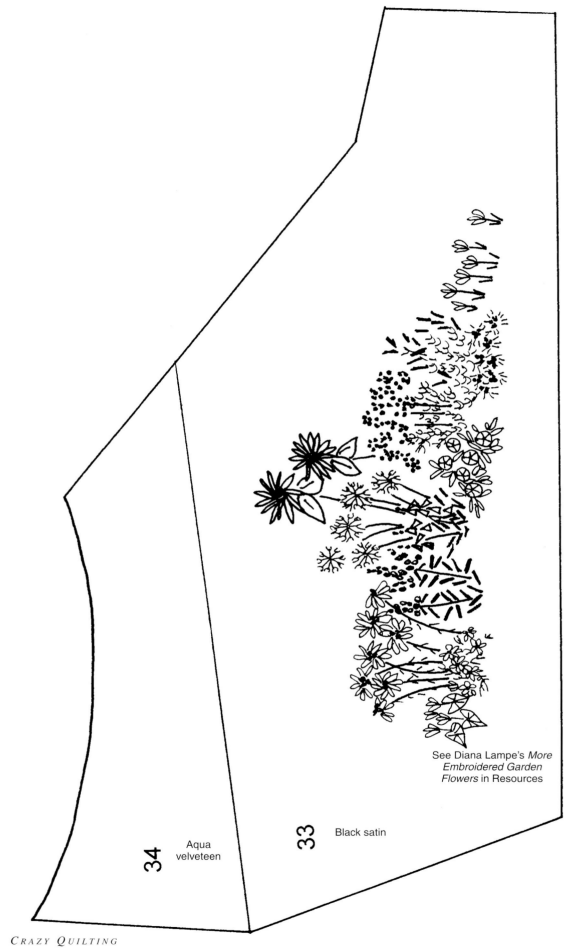

See Diana Lampe's *More Embroidered Garden Flowers* in Resources

34 Aqua velveteen

33 Black satin

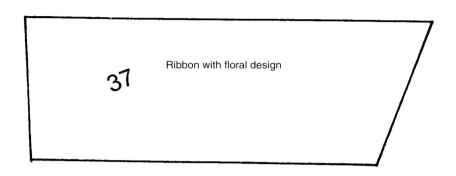

37   Ribbon with floral design

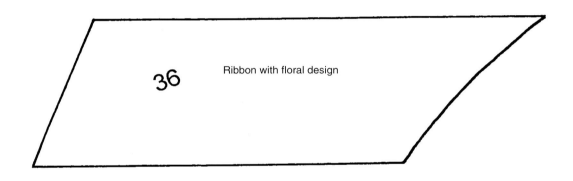

36   Ribbon with floral design

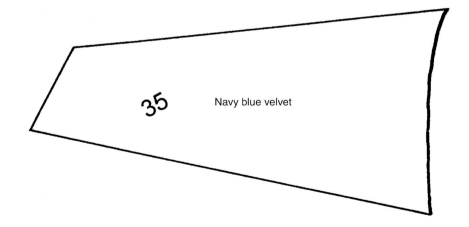

35   Navy blue velvet

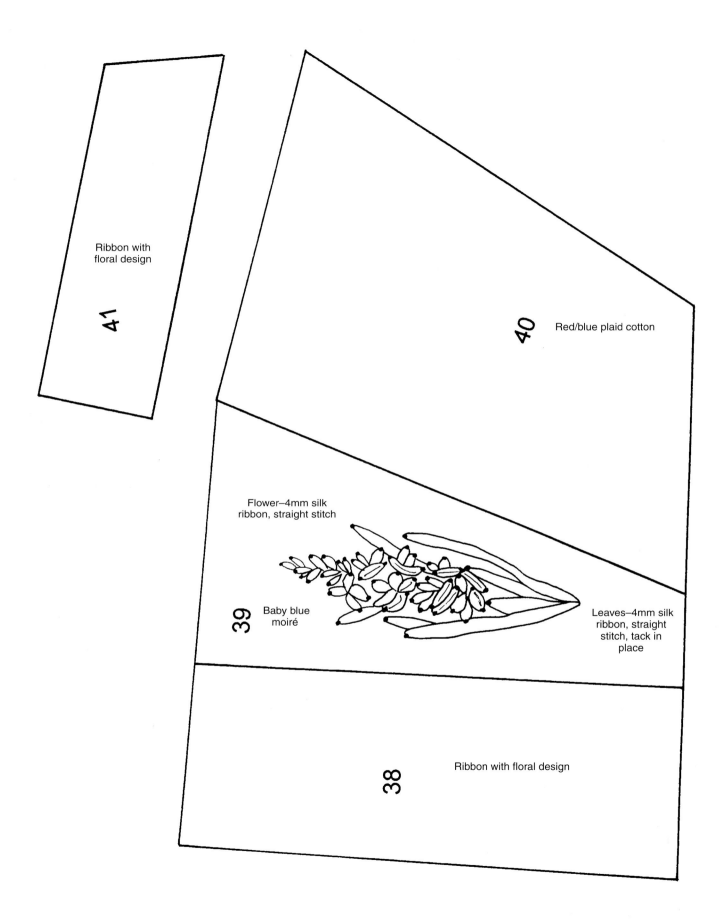

Ribbon with
floral design

41

40 Red/blue plaid cotton

Flower—4mm silk
ribbon, straight stitch

39 Baby blue
moiré

Leaves—4mm silk
ribbon, straight
stitch, tack in
place

38 Ribbon with floral design

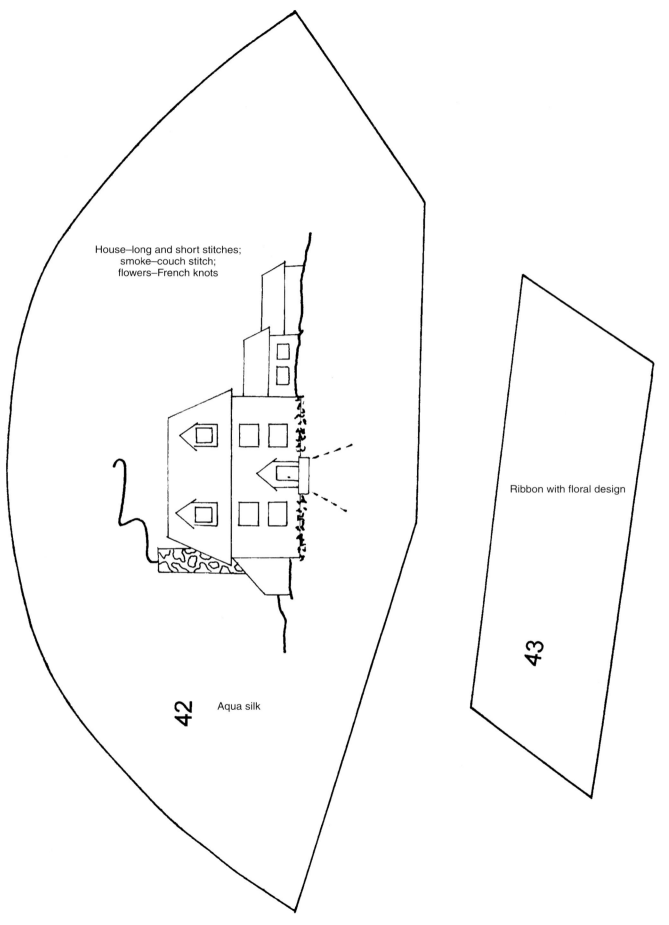

House—long and short stitches;
smoke—couch stitch;
flowers—French knots

42   Aqua silk

Ribbon with floral design

43

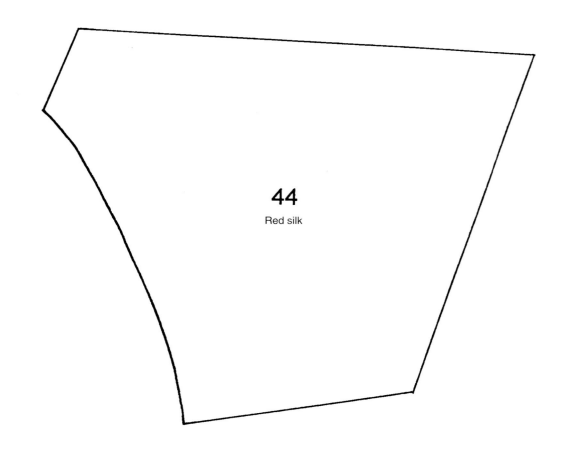

44

Red silk

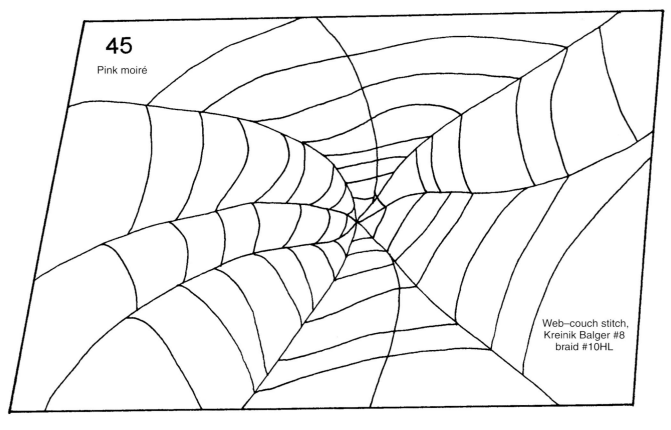

45

Pink moiré

Web–couch stitch,
Kreinik Balger #8
braid #10HL

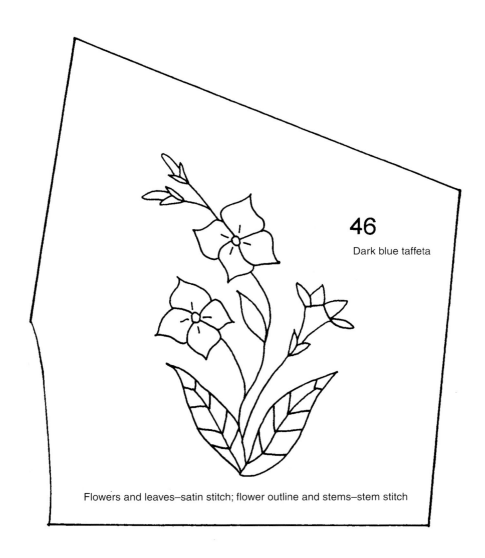

46

Dark blue taffeta

Flowers and leaves–satin stitch; flower outline and stems–stem stitch

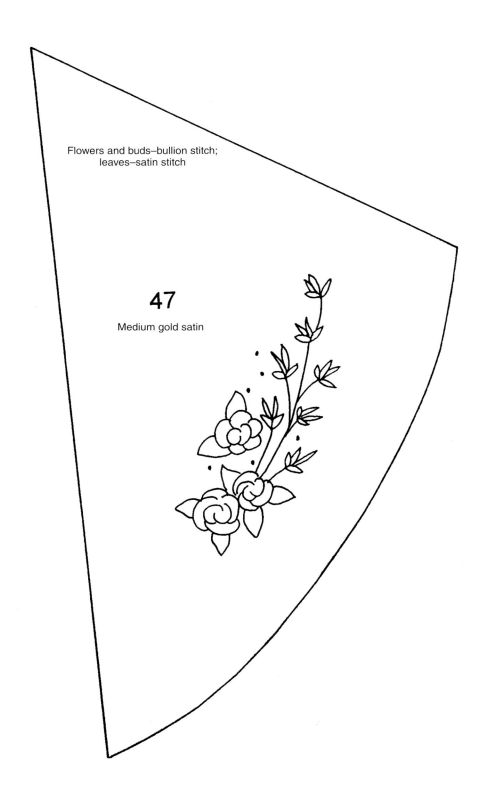

Flowers and buds—bullion stitch;
leaves—satin stitch

47

Medium gold satin

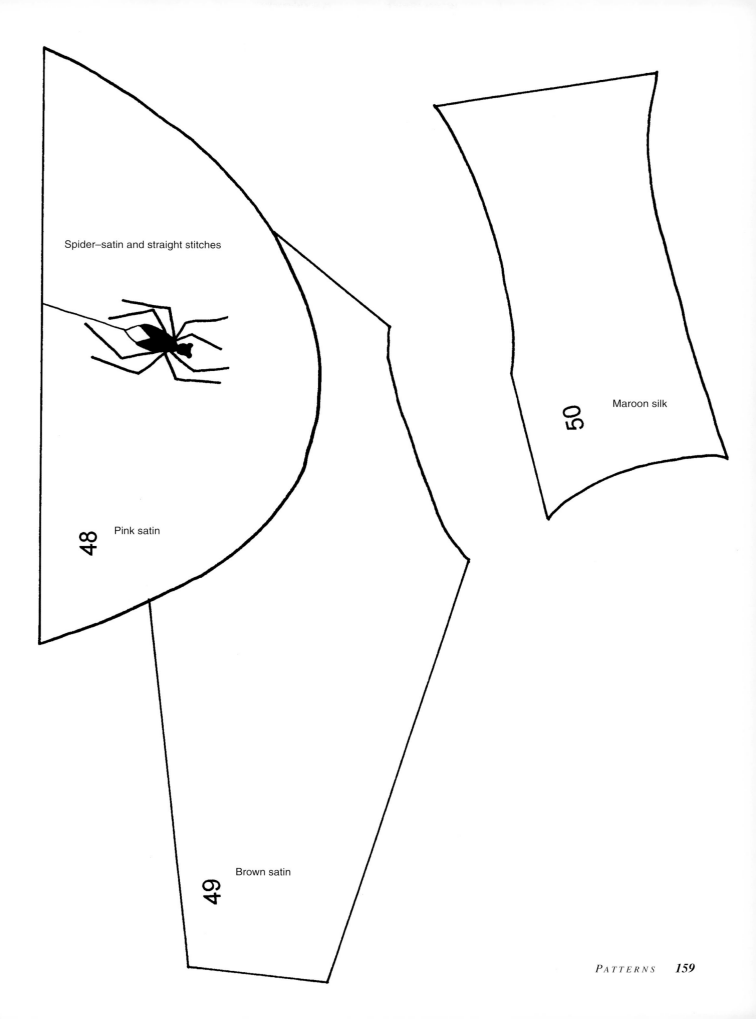

Spider—satin and straight stitches

48 Pink satin

49 Brown satin

50 Maroon silk

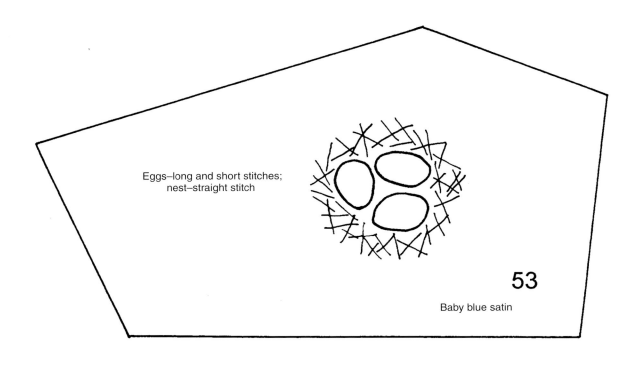

Eggs–long and short stitches;
nest–straight stitch

53

Baby blue satin

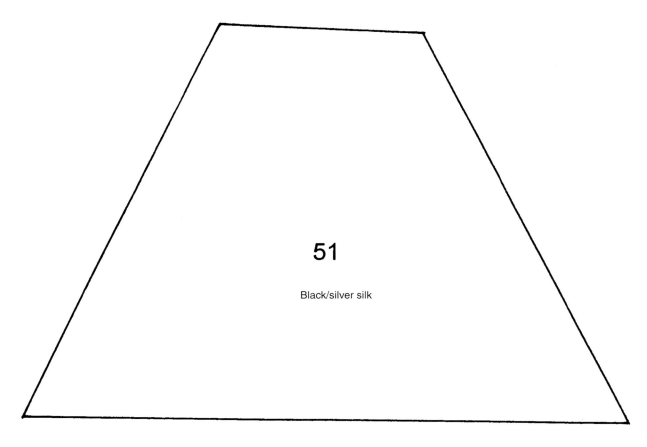

51

Black/silver silk

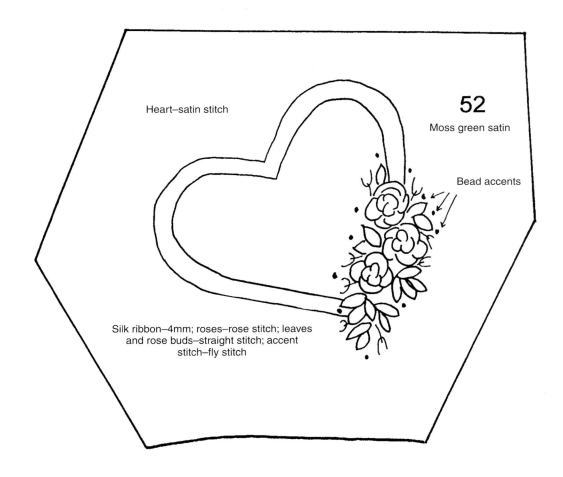

Heart–satin stitch

52

Moss green satin

Bead accents

Silk ribbon–4mm; roses–rose stitch; leaves
and rose buds–straight stitch; accent
stitch–fly stitch

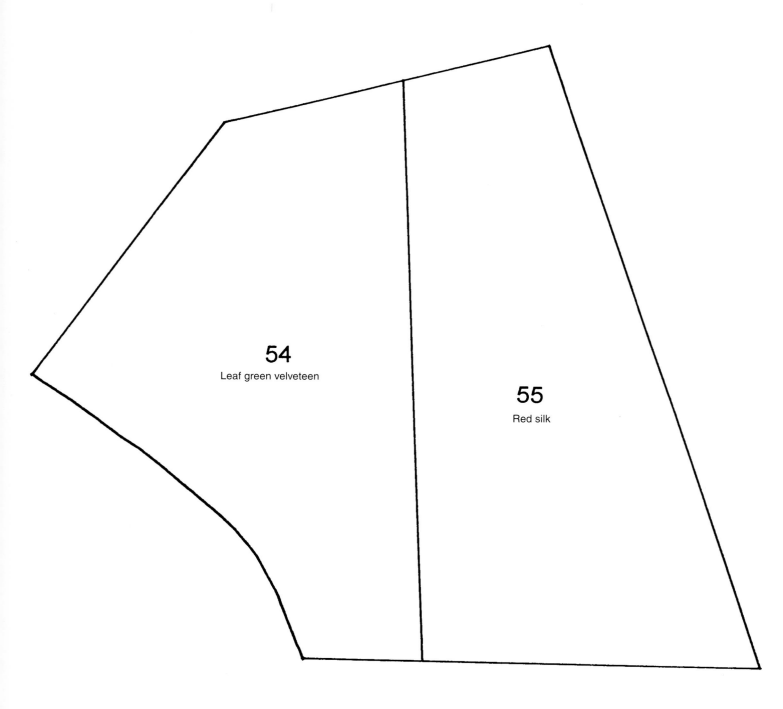

54
Leaf green velveteen

55
Red silk

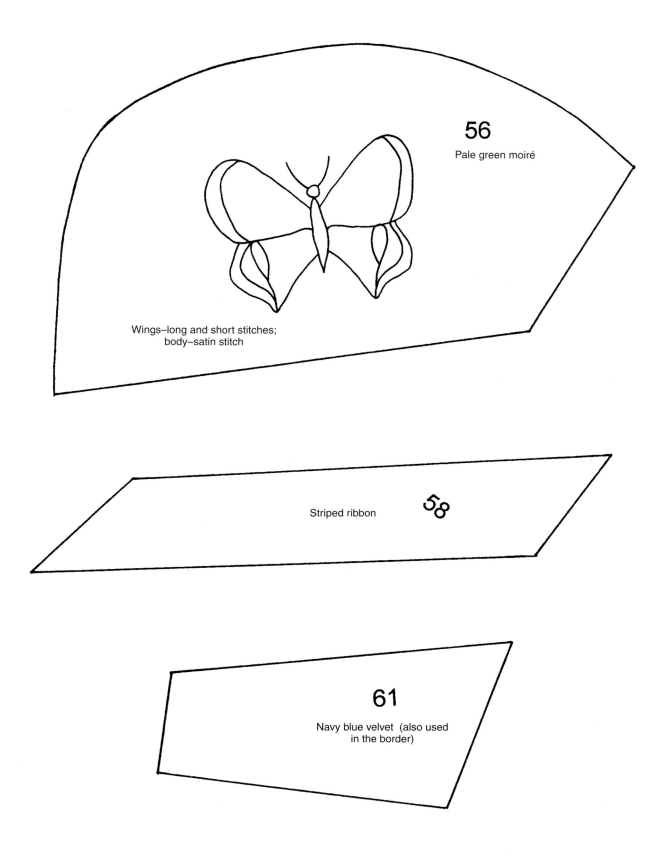

56

Pale green moiré

Wings–long and short stitches;
body–satin stitch

Striped ribbon   58

61

Navy blue velvet (also used
in the border)

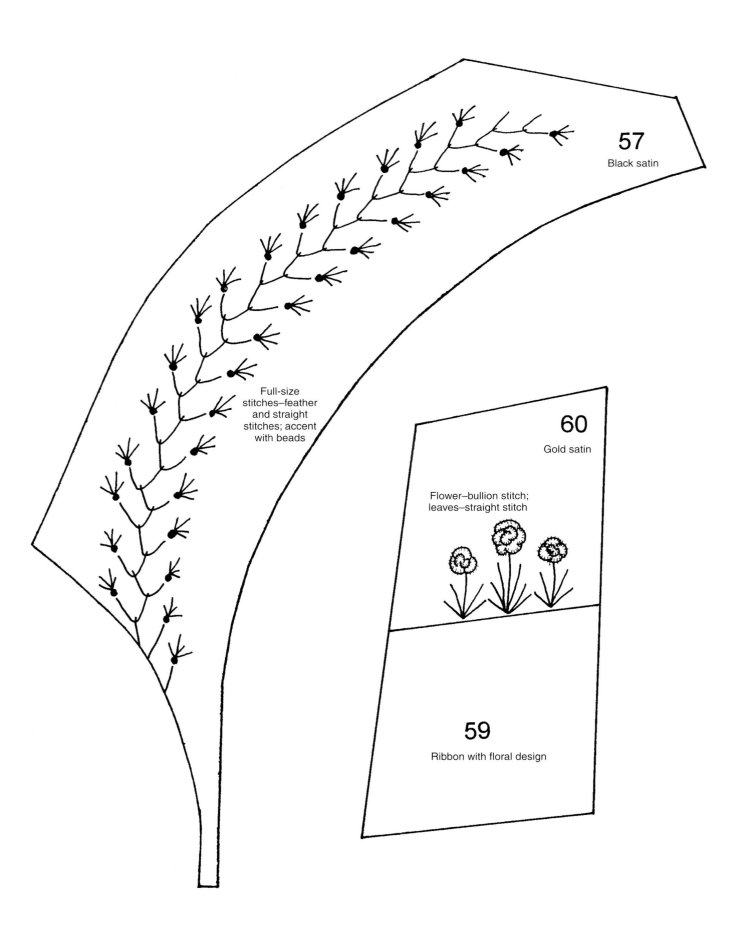

57

Black satin

Full-size
stitches—feather
and straight
stitches; accent
with beads

60

Gold satin

Flower—bullion stitch;
leaves—straight stitch

59

Ribbon with floral design

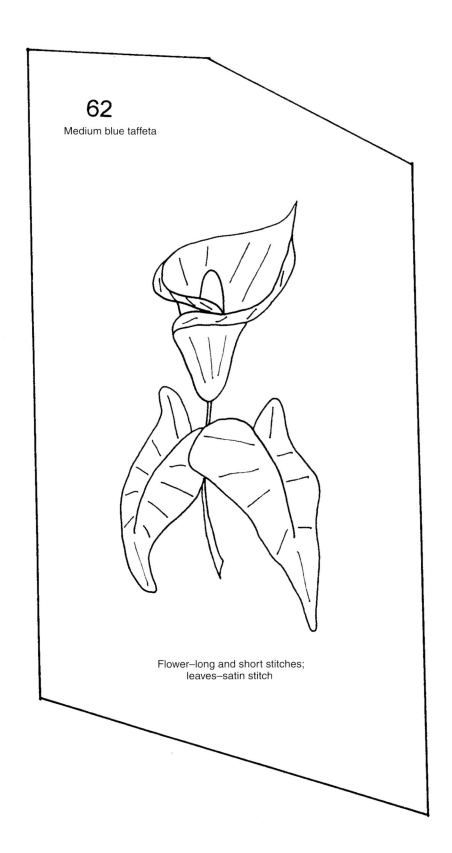

62

Medium blue taffeta

Flower–long and short stitches;
leaves–satin stitch

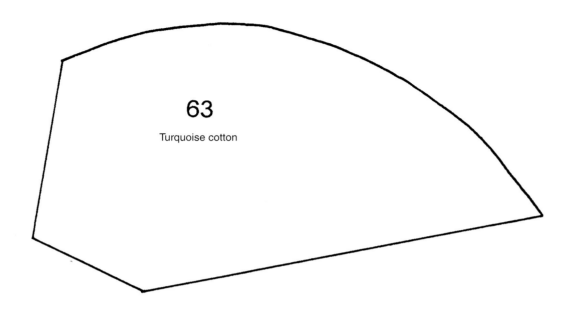

63

Turquoise cotton

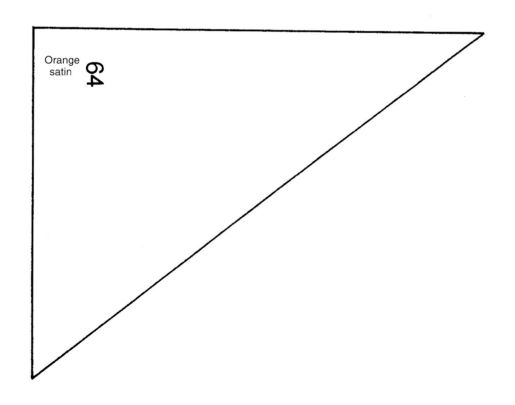

Orange
satin

64

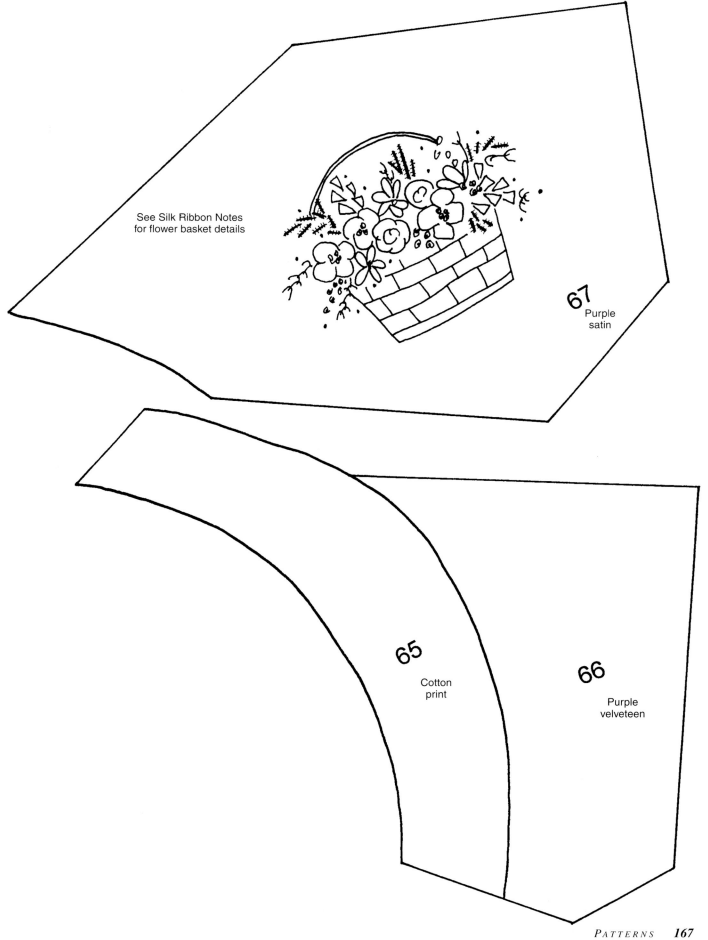

See Silk Ribbon Notes
for flower basket details

67
Purple
satin

65

Cotton
print

66

Purple
velveteen

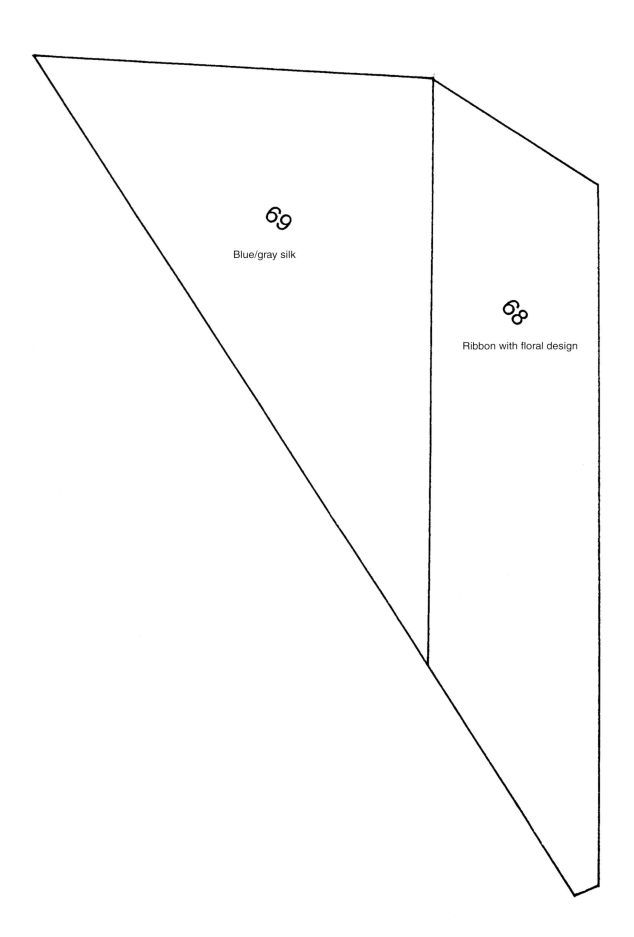

69

Blue/gray silk

68

Ribbon with floral design

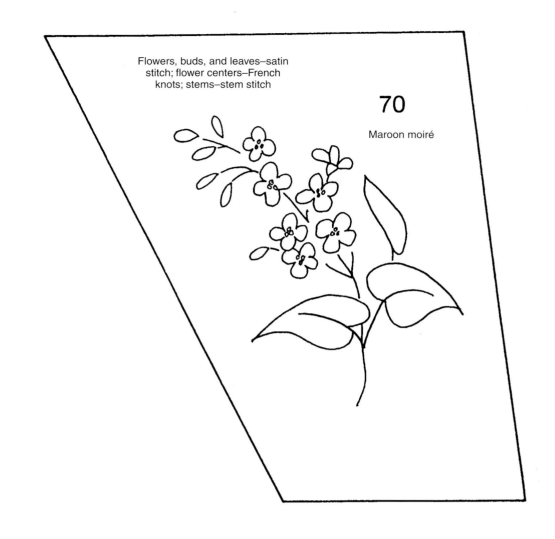

Flowers, buds, and leaves–satin
stitch; flower centers–French
knots; stems–stem stitch

70

Maroon moiré

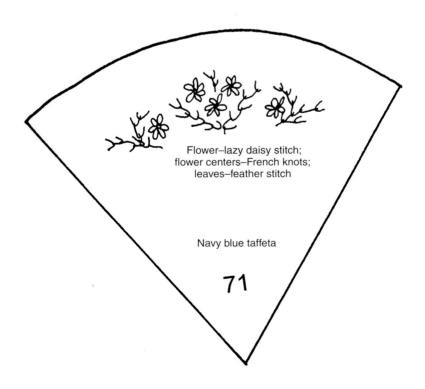

Flower–lazy daisy stitch;
flower centers–French knots;
leaves–feather stitch

Navy blue taffeta

71

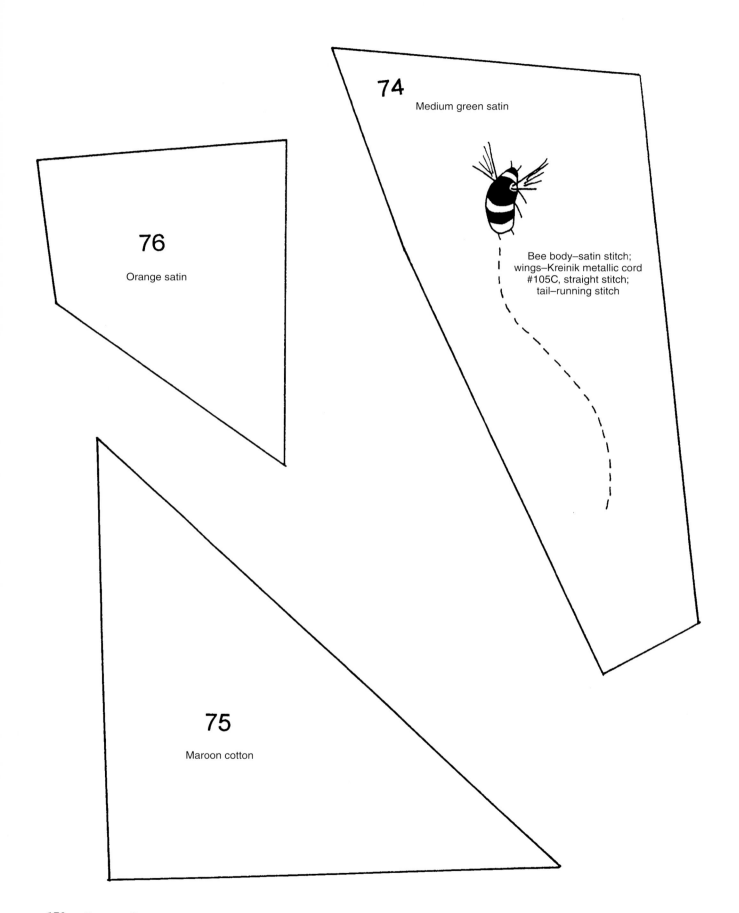

74

Medium green satin

Bee body–satin stitch; wings–Kreinik metallic cord #105C, straight stitch; tail–running stitch

76

Orange satin

75

Maroon cotton

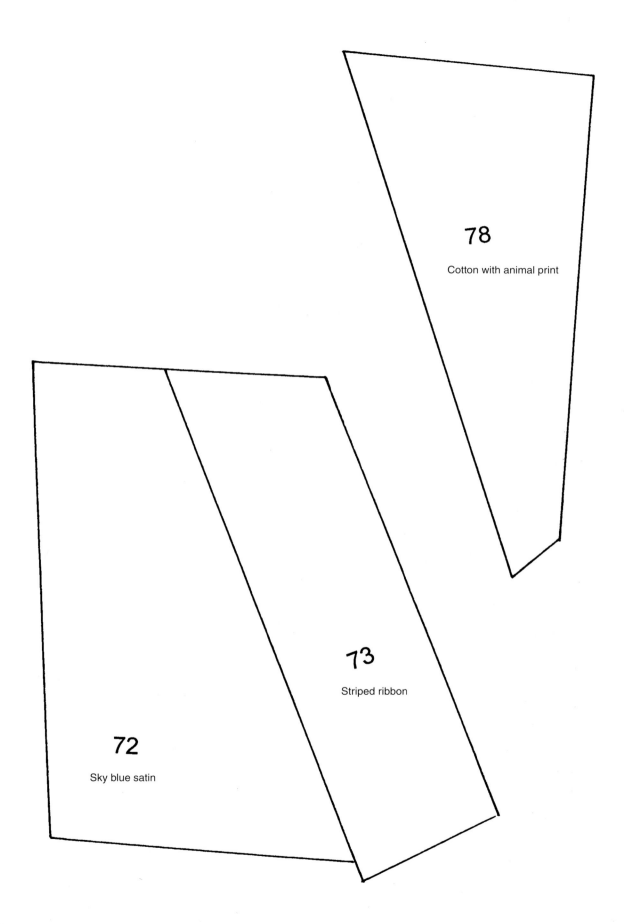

78

Cotton with animal print

73

Striped ribbon

72

Sky blue satin

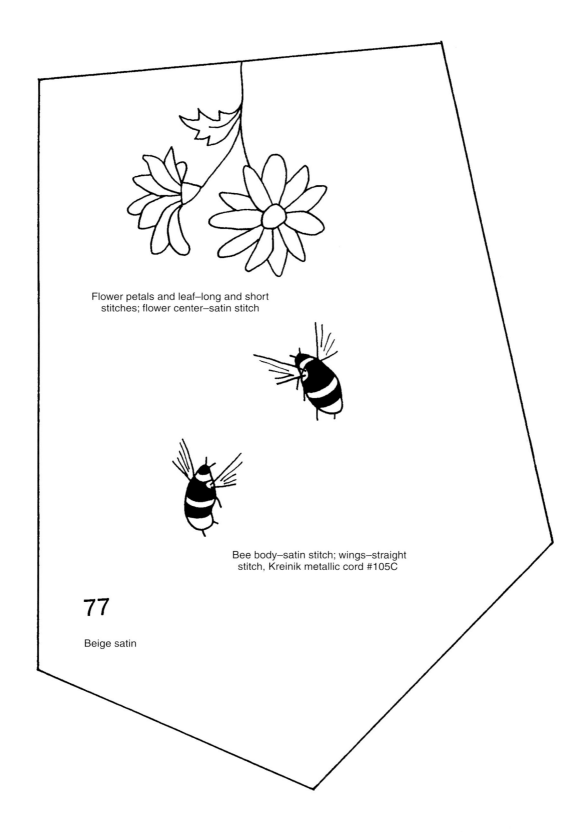

Flower petals and leaf–long and short
stitches; flower center–satin stitch

Bee body–satin stitch; wings–straight
stitch, Kreinik metallic cord #105C

77

Beige satin

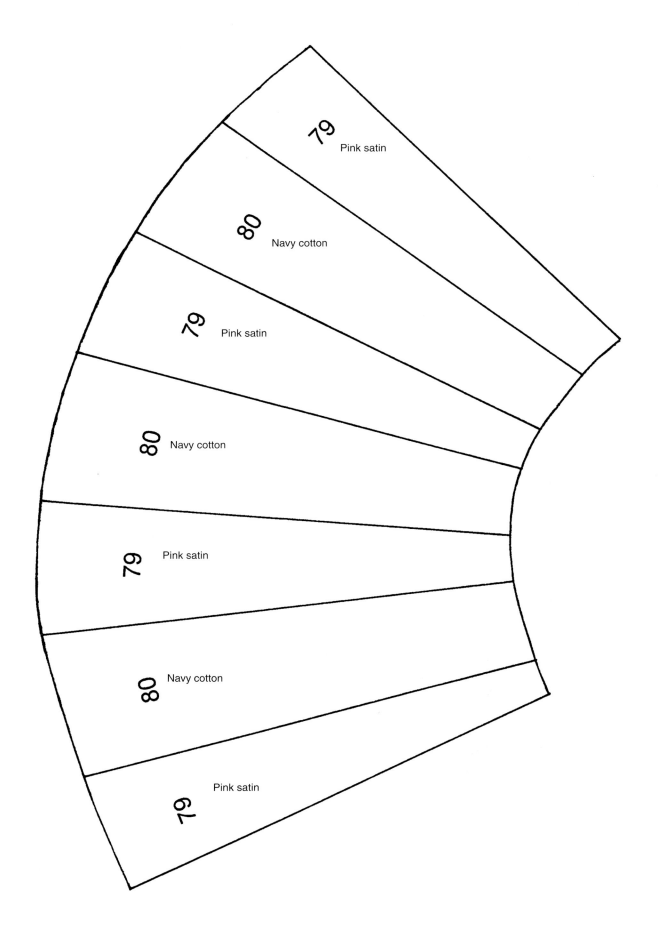

79 Pink satin

80 Navy cotton

79 Pink satin

80 Navy cotton

79 Pink satin

80 Navy cotton

79 Pink satin

DECORATIVE SEAM COVERINGS STITCH GUIDE

All stitches are shown actual size; each decorative seam covering is accented with beads.

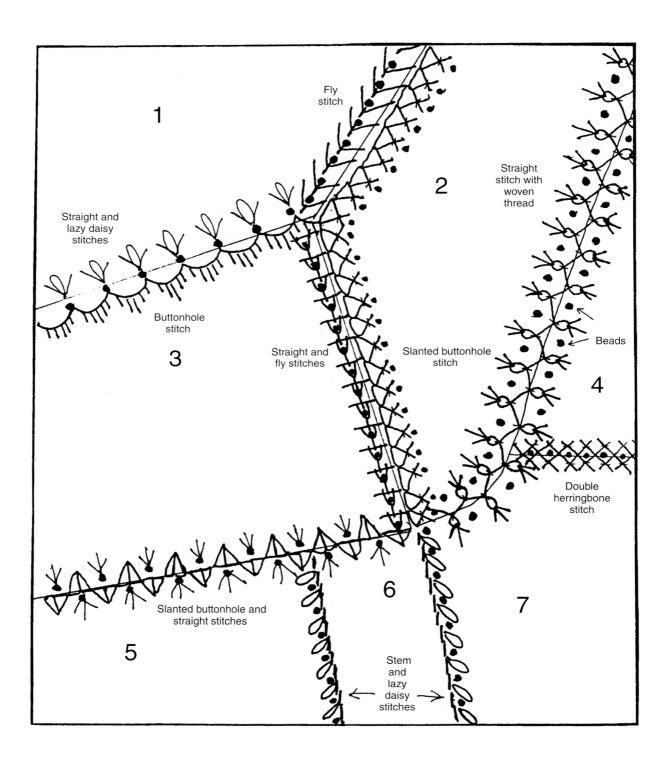

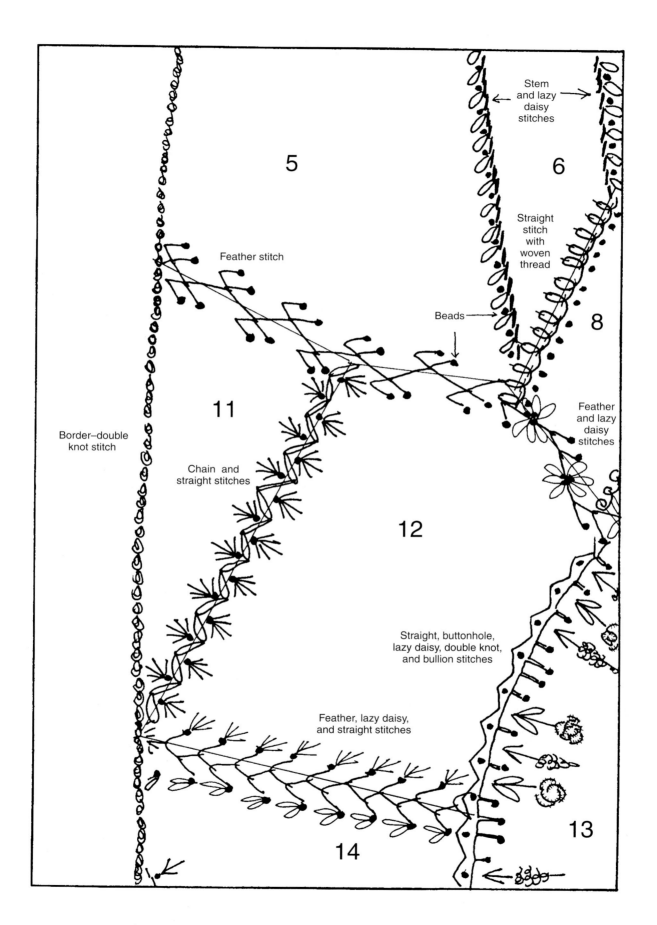

5

6

Stem and lazy daisy stitches

Straight stitch with woven thread

Feather stitch

Beads

8

11

Border–double knot stitch

Feather and lazy daisy stitches

Chain and straight stitches

12

Straight, buttonhole, lazy daisy, double knot, and bullion stitches

Feather, lazy daisy, and straight stitches

13

14

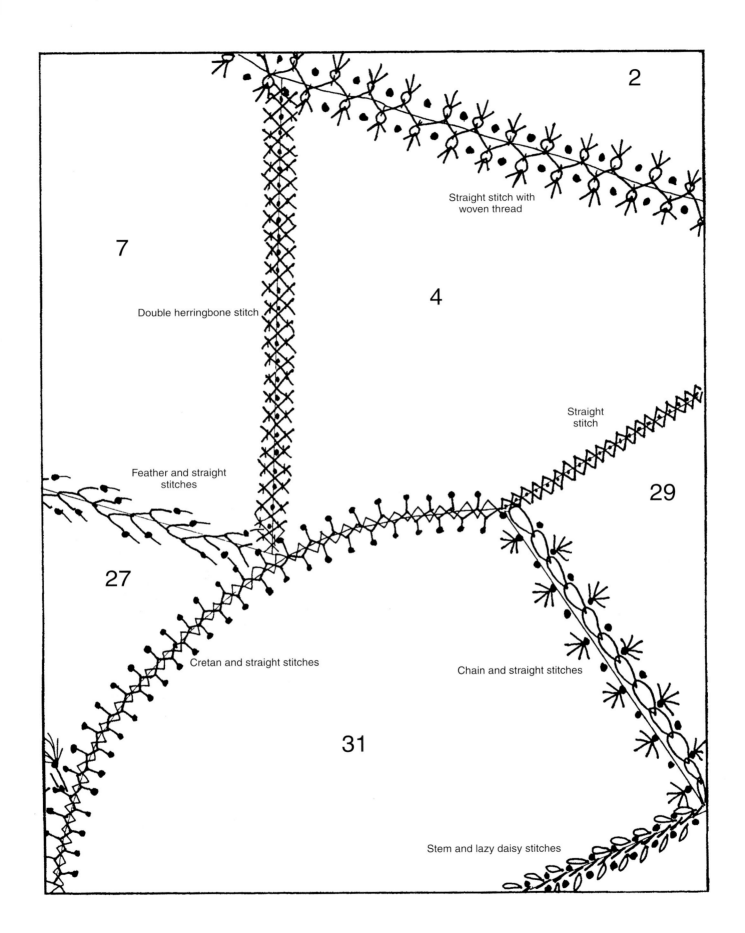

2

Straight stitch with
woven thread

7

Double herringbone stitch

4

Straight
stitch

Feather and straight
stitches

29

27

Cretan and straight stitches

Chain and straight stitches

31

Stem and lazy daisy stitches

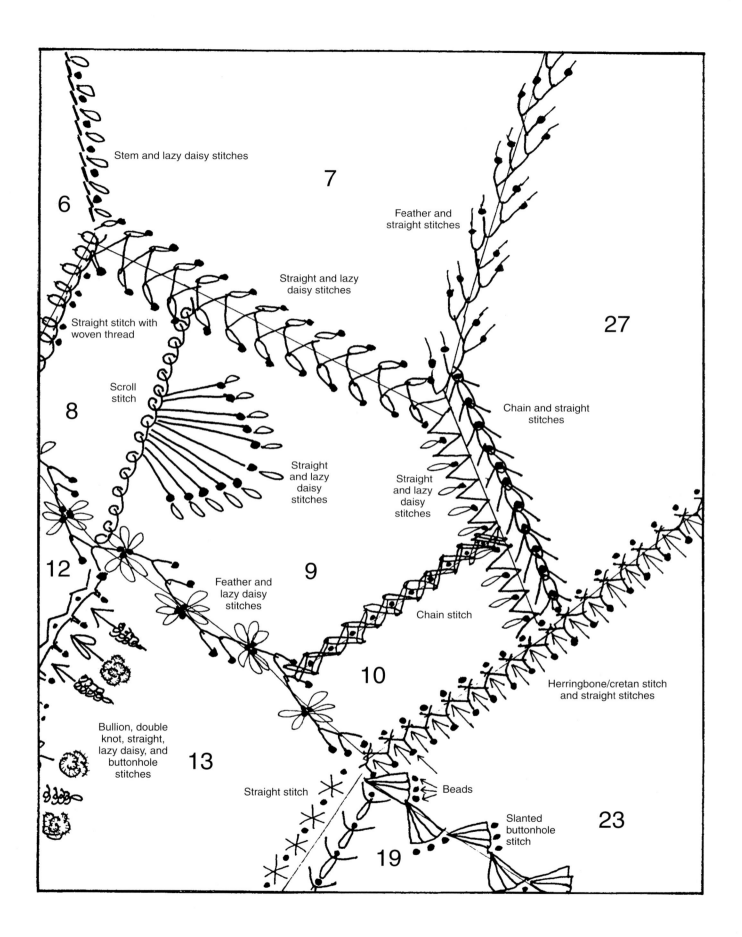

Stem and lazy daisy stitches

6

7

Feather and straight stitches

27

Straight and lazy daisy stitches

Straight stitch with woven thread

Scroll stitch

8

Straight and lazy daisy stitches

Chain and straight stitches

Straight and lazy daisy stitches

12

9

Feather and lazy daisy stitches

Chain stitch

10

Herringbone/cretan stitch and straight stitches

Bullion, double knot, straight, lazy daisy, and buttonhole stitches

13

Straight stitch

Beads

Slanted buttonhole stitch

23

19

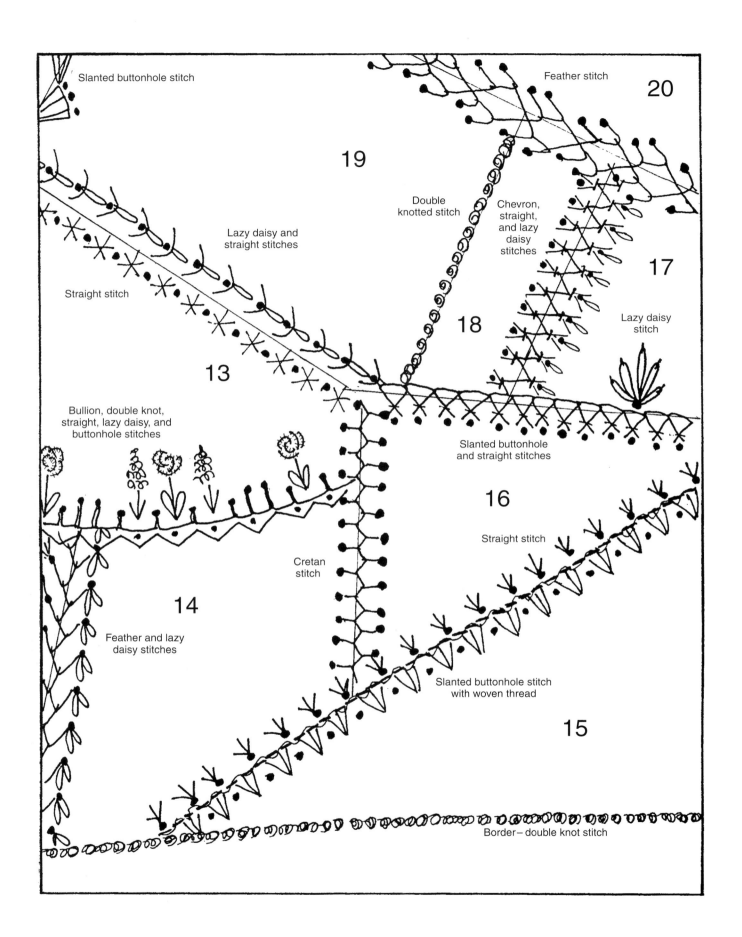

Slanted buttonhole stitch

Feather stitch

20

19

Double knotted stitch

Chevron, straight, and lazy daisy stitches

Lazy daisy and straight stitches

17

Straight stitch

18

Lazy daisy stitch

13

Bullion, double knot, straight, lazy daisy, and buttonhole stitches

Slanted buttonhole and straight stitches

16

Straight stitch

Cretan stitch

14

Feather and lazy daisy stitches

Slanted buttonhole stitch with woven thread

15

Border – double knot stitch

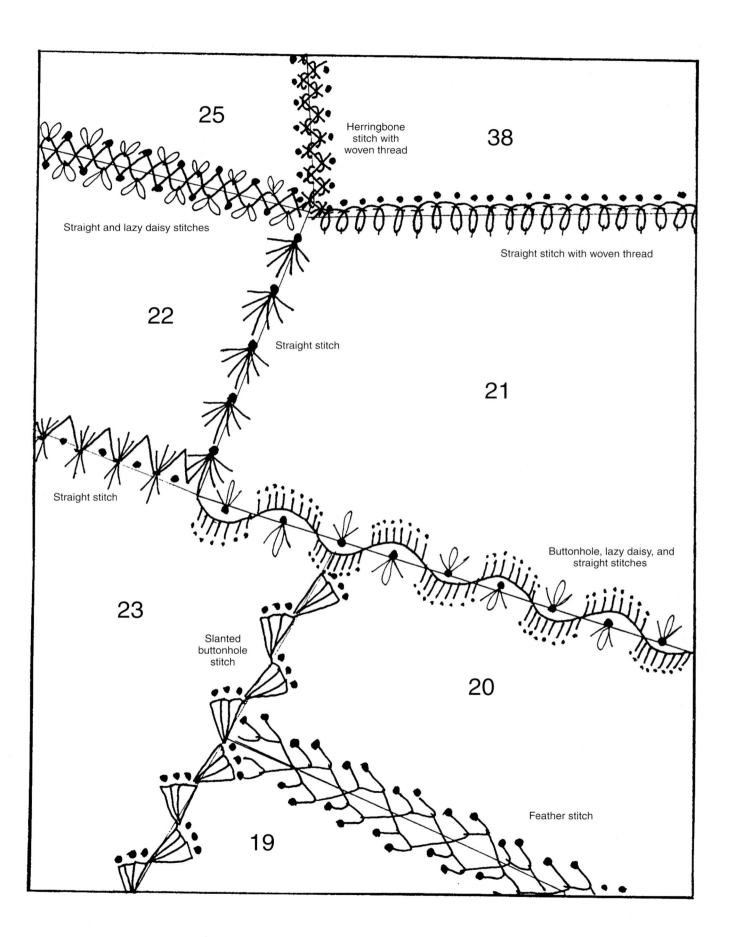

25

Herringbone
stitch with
woven thread

38

Straight and lazy daisy stitches

Straight stitch with woven thread

22

Straight stitch

21

Straight stitch

Buttonhole, lazy daisy, and
straight stitches

23

Slanted
buttonhole
stitch

20

19

Feather stitch

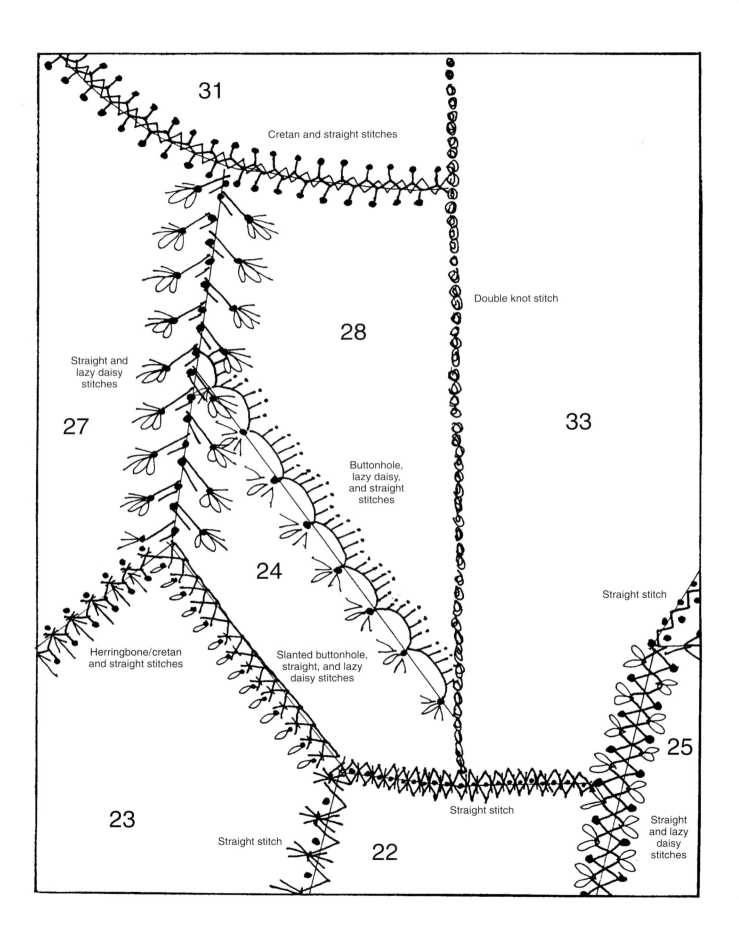

31

Cretan and straight stitches

Double knot stitch

28

Straight and
lazy daisy
stitches

27

Buttonhole,
lazy daisy,
and straight
stitches

33

24

Straight stitch

Herringbone/cretan
and straight stitches

Slanted buttonhole,
straight, and lazy
daisy stitches

25

23

Straight stitch

22

Straight stitch

Straight
and lazy
daisy
stitches

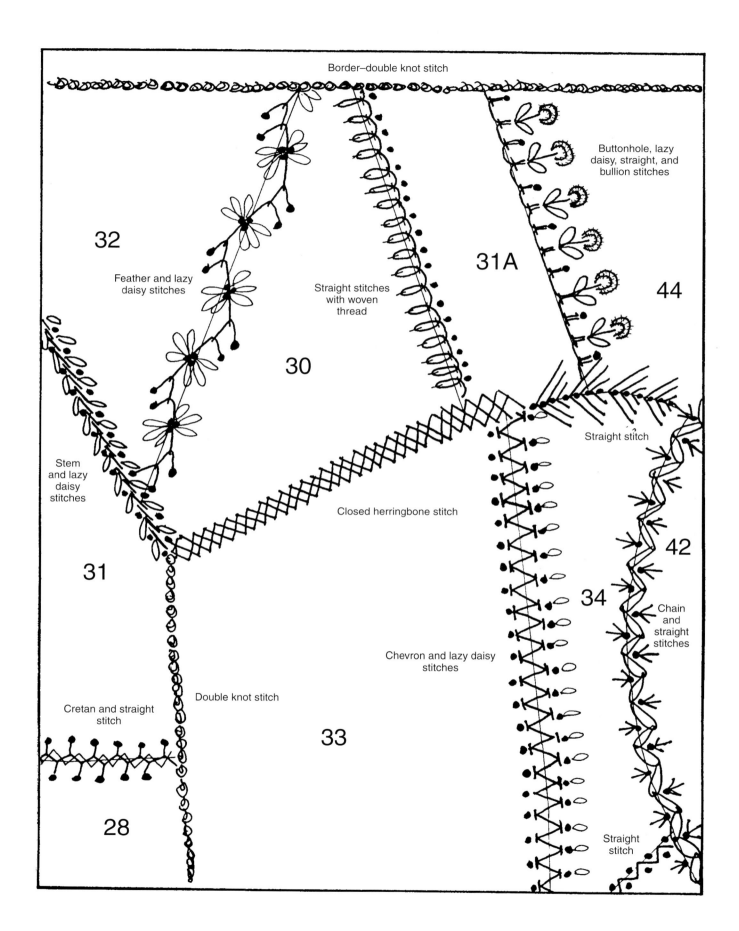

Border—double knot stitch

32

Feather and lazy
daisy stitches

31A

Buttonhole, lazy
daisy, straight, and
bullion stitches

44

Straight stitches
with woven
thread

30

Stem
and lazy
daisy
stitches

Straight stitch

Closed herringbone stitch

42

31

34

Chain
and
straight
stitches

Cretan and straight
stitch

Double knot stitch

Chevron and lazy daisy
stitches

33

28

Straight
stitch

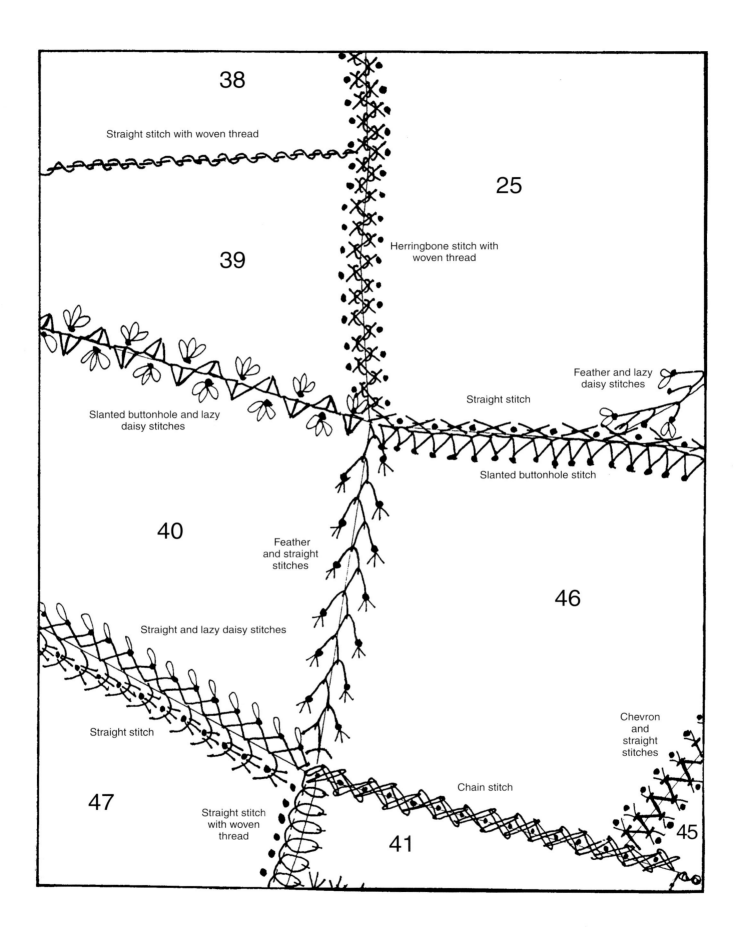

38

Straight stitch with woven thread

25

39

Herringbone stitch with woven thread

Feather and lazy daisy stitches

Straight stitch

Slanted buttonhole and lazy daisy stitches

Slanted buttonhole stitch

40

Feather and straight stitches

46

Straight and lazy daisy stitches

Straight stitch

Chevron and straight stitches

47

Straight stitch with woven thread

Chain stitch

41

45

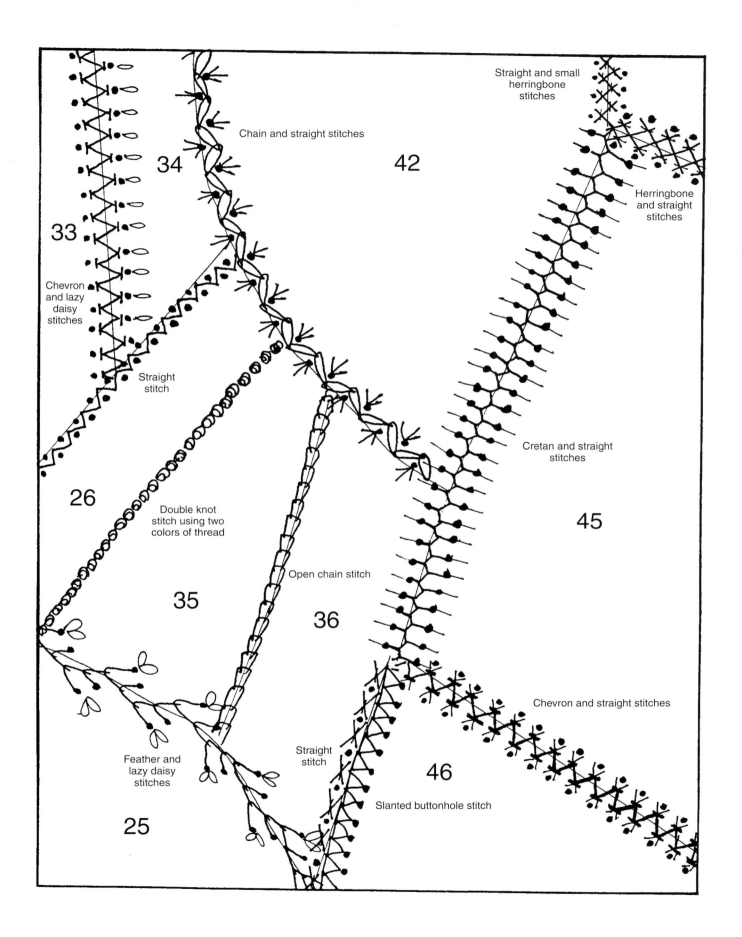

Straight and small
herringbone
stitches

Chain and straight stitches

42

33

34

Herringbone
and straight
stitches

Chevron
and lazy
daisy
stitches

Straight
stitch

26

Cretan and straight
stitches

Double knot
stitch using two
colors of thread

45

Open chain stitch

35

36

Chevron and straight stitches

Feather and
lazy daisy
stitches

Straight
stitch

46

25

Slanted buttonhole stitch

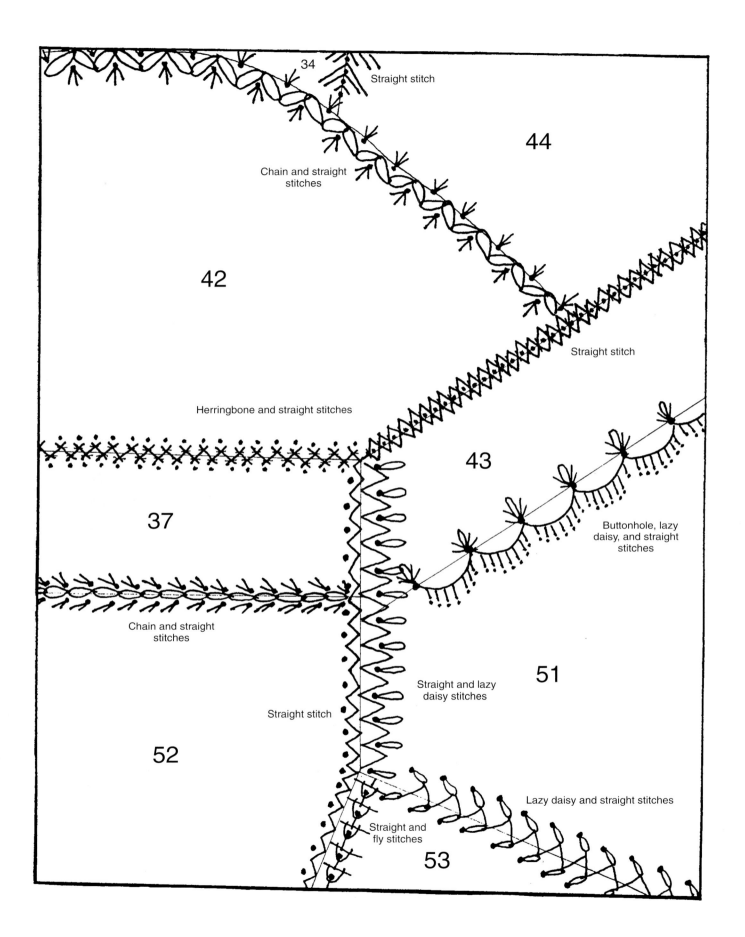

34

Straight stitch

44

Chain and straight
stitches

42

Straight stitch

Herringbone and straight stitches

43

37

Buttonhole, lazy
daisy, and straight
stitches

Chain and straight
stitches

51

Straight and lazy
daisy stitches

Straight stitch

52

Lazy daisy and straight stitches

Straight and
fly stitches

53

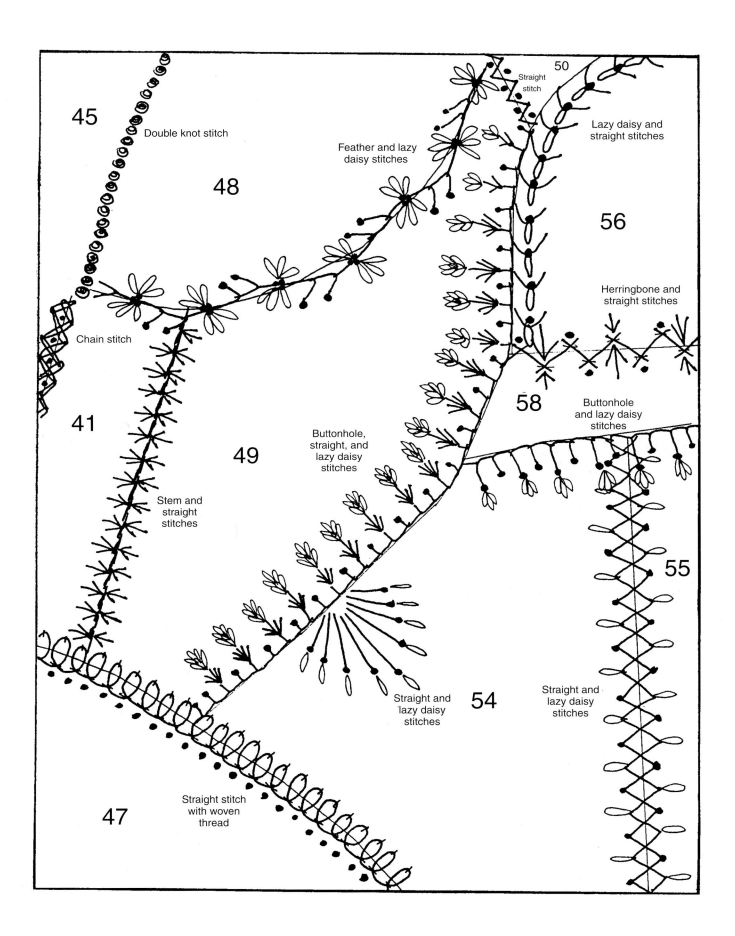

45 Double knot stitch

48

50 Straight stitch

Lazy daisy and straight stitches

Feather and lazy daisy stitches

56

Herringbone and straight stitches

Chain stitch

41

49

Buttonhole, straight, and lazy daisy stitches

58 Buttonhole and lazy daisy stitches

Stem and straight stitches

55

Straight and lazy daisy stitches

Straight and lazy daisy stitches

54

47 Straight stitch with woven thread

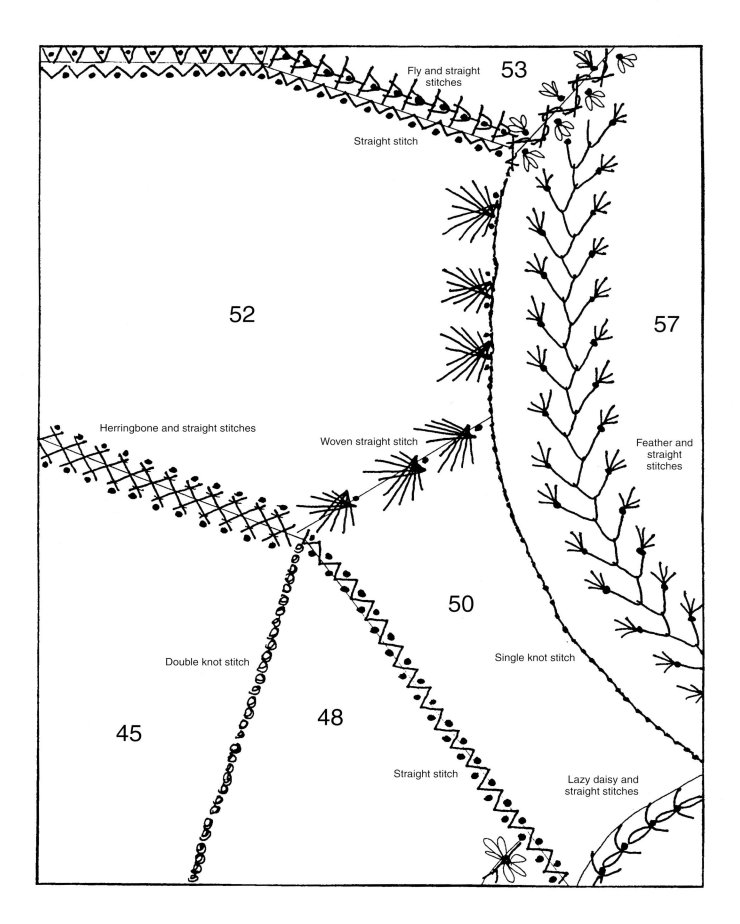

Fly and straight
stitches

53

Straight stitch

52

57

Herringbone and straight stitches

Woven straight stitch

Feather and
straight
stitches

Double knot stitch

50

Single knot stitch

45

48

Straight stitch

Lazy daisy and
straight stitches

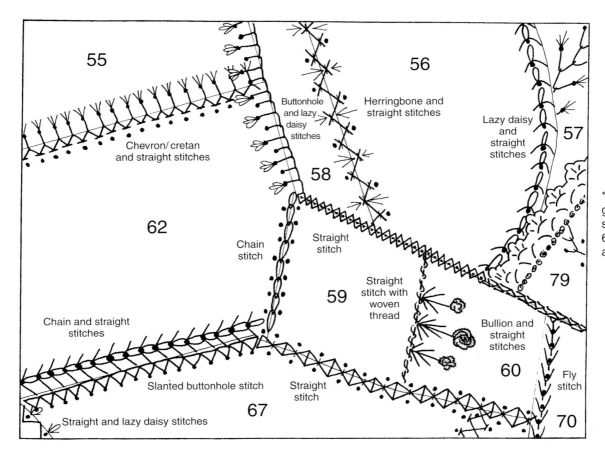

55

Chevron/cretan
and straight stitches

Buttonhole
and lazy
daisy
stitches

56

Herringbone and
straight stitches

Lazy daisy
and
straight
stitches

57

58

62

Chain
stitch

Straight
stitch

Straight
stitch with
woven
thread

59

79

Chain and straight
stitches

Bullion and
straight
stitches

60

Slanted buttonhole stitch

Straight
stitch

Fly
stitch

Straight and lazy daisy stitches

67

70

*This stitch
guide is
shown at
65% of
actual size.

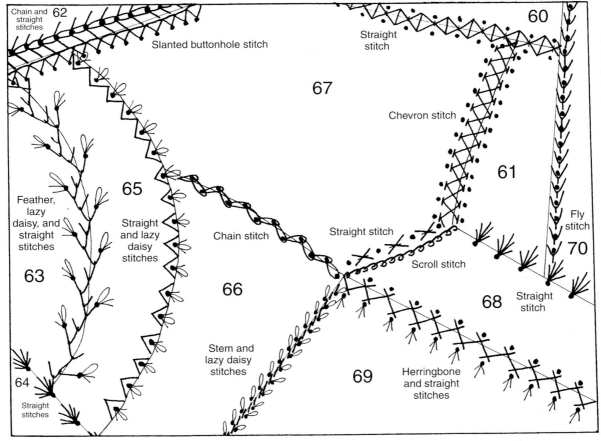

Chain and
straight
stitches

62

60

Slanted buttonhole stitch

Straight
stitch

67

Chevron stitch

61

Feather,
lazy
daisy, and
straight
stitches

65

Straight
and lazy
daisy
stitches

Chain stitch

Straight stitch

Fly
stitch

70

63

66

Scroll stitch

Straight
stitch

68

64

Stem and
lazy daisy
stitches

69

Herringbone
and straight
stitches

Straight
stitches

*This stitch
guide is
shown at
65% of
actual size.

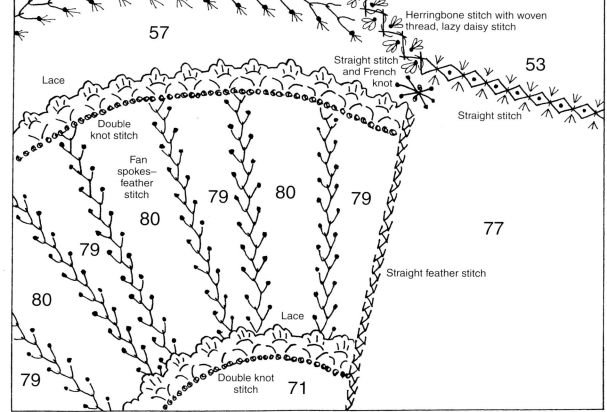

Double knot stitch

71

Straight feather stitch

70

Straight stitch

Bullion, buttonhole, and double knot stitches; French knot

73

Chain stitch

72

Straight stitch

68

Straight stitch

77

74

CD 1995

76

Buttonhole and straight stitches; lettering–stem stitch

Cretan stitch

78

Straight and slanted buttonhole stitches

Feather stitch

75

*This stitch guide is shown at 65% of actual size.

57

Lace

Double knot stitch

Fan spokes– feather stitch

80

79

80

79

80

80

79

79

79

Lace

Double knot stitch

71

Herringbone stitch with woven thread, lazy daisy stitch

Straight stitch and French knot

53

Straight stitch

77

Straight feather stitch

*This stitch guide is shown at 65% of actual size.

Glossary of Terms

Appliqué—a single, cutout piece of fabric stitched onto the surface of another fabric for decoration.

Batting—blanket-like filling made from cotton, wool, silk, or synthetic fibers.

Border—narrow fabric panels used to frame a crazy patch.

Chalk pencil—pencil with a chalk center. (I recommend Clover Chacopel Fine pencils for fabric marking, available in yellow, white, pink, and blue at most quilt shops.)

Crazy quilt—quilt made from a variety of fabrics placed in a random manner, with embroidered patches and seams covered in decorative stitches.

Diagonal—a line extending from a top corner to the farthest opposite lower corner.

Embroidery—the art of stitching an ornamental design on fabric in threads of silk, cotton, etc.

Embroidery hoop—round or oval wooden or plastic double hoop used to hold fabric taut.

Finger press—pressing or creasing a piece of folded fabric between two fingers.

Foundation—fabric that serves as a base on which to sew crazy patches.

Layers—the quilt top, batting, and backing.

Motif—a design outline that can be painted or embroidered.

Provenance—origin and/or history of ownership of a particular quilt.

Quilt backing—the fabric back of a quilt.

Rice paper—a thin, lightweight, pliable material that resembles paper.

Silk ribbon—delicate lightweight ribbon most often available in 2-, 4-, and 7-millimeter widths. (See Resources.)

Stab stitch—method in which needle is passed straight down from the quilt top to the back, sewing one stitch at a time.

Tacking—the stitching used to secure the quilt layers together at intervals of 4 to 6 inches.

Template—pattern shape cut from poster board. (Poster board can be purchased at art supply stores.)

Tracing paper—a see-through paper used to copy a design. (Available at art supply stores.)

Transfer paper—a carbon-like paper that, when drawn upon, leaves the image on a fabric surface. (I recommend Saral® transfer paper, available at art supply stores.)

Tying—a method of securing quilt layers together with knots, usually tied at the back of the quilt.

Resources

SUPPLIES

AK Designs
3815-A East Thousand Oaks Blvd.
Thousand Oaks, California 91362
Phone: 805-497-9844
Fax: 805-497-8103
Petite and seed beads, Nymo® thread and supplies. Contact local needlepoint and hobby/craft shops for beads and beading supplies.

The DMC Corporation
South Hackensack Avenue
Port Kearny Building 10A
South Kearny, New Jersey 07032
DMC embroidery floss and pearl cotton threads. Contact local needlepoint and hobby/craft shops for DMC threads.

Jukebox/Galloping Rabbit Press
P.O. Box 1518
Tustin, California 92781-1518
Phone: 714-731-2563
Fax: 714-505-4677
E-mail: Kelly_jukebox@msn.com
Crazy quilt patterns, books, glass beads, quilt patterns, and supplies.

The Kirk Collection
1513 Military Avenue
Omaha, Nebraska 68111
Phone: 1-800-398-2542 or 402-551-0386
Fax: 1-800-960-8335 or 402-551-0971
E-mail: KirkColl@aol.com
Website: www.kirkcollection.com
Specializing in fabrics, lace, trims and embellishments for crazy quilts. Contact for Pigma pens and Clover chalk pencils.

Kreinik Mfg. Co., Inc.
3106 Timanus Lane, Suite 101
Baltimore, Maryland 21244
Phone: 1-800-537-2166
Kreinik silk and metallic threads. Contact local needlepoint shops for Kreinik threads.

Photos-To-Fabric™
Ami Simms
Mallery Press
4206 Sheraton Drive
Flint, Michigan 48532-3557
Phone: 1-800-A-Stitch or 810-733-8743
Fax: 810-230-1516
E-mail: amisimms@aol.com
Photo-transfer paper and complete instructions for transferring photos to fabric.

Prym Dritz® Corporation
Spartanburg, South Carolina 29304
Dritz® Fray Check™ stops fabric from fraying. Available in yardage, quilt, or craft shops.

Saral® Paper Corporation
436-D Central Avenue
Bohemia, New York 11716
Wax free Saral® transfer paper available in graphite, red, blue, white, and yellow. Excellent transfer paper for transferring motifs to fabric. Contact local art supply stores.

The Warm Company
954 East Union Street
Seattle, Washington 98122
Phone: 1-800-234-9276 or 206 320-9276
Fax: 206-320-0974
Website: www.warmcompany.com
Cotton and wool batting. Contact local yardage and quilt specialty shops.

YLI Corporation
P.O. Box 109
Provo, Utah 84603
Phone: 1-800-854-1932
Silk ribbon and supplies. Contact needlepoint, quilt, and craft shops for silk ribbon.

INSTRUCTIONAL

Bond, Dorothy
Crazy Quilt Stitches
ISBN 0-9606086-0-5
Cottage Grove, Oregon
1981

Bradford, Jenny
Textured Embroidery
Sally Milner Publishing Pty. Ltd.
Burra Creek, NSW, Australia
1993

Montano, Judith
The Crazy Quilt Handbook
C&T Publishing
Lafayette, California
1986

Newman, Jennifer
Exquisite Embroidery
Sally Milner Publishing Pty. Ltd.
Burra Creek, NSW, Australia
1993

Ryan, Mildred Graves
The Complete Encyclopedia of Stitchery
Doubleday Book & Music Clubs
New York, New York
1979

Snook, Barbara
Embroidery Stitches
St. Martin's Press, Inc.
New York, New York
1986

SILK RIBBON EMBROIDERY

Bradford, Jenny
Silk Ribbon Embroidery for Gifts and Garments
Sally Milner Publishing Pty. Ltd.
Burra Creek, NSW, Australia
1990

Bradford, Jenny
Original Designs for Silk Ribbon Embroidery
Sally Milner Publishing Pty. Ltd.
Burra Creek, NSW, Australia
1991

MacDonald, Robbyn
Victorian Embroidery
Sally Milner Publishing Pty. Ltd.
Burra Creek, NSW, Australia
1993

Newman, Jennifer
Exquisite Embroidery
Sally Milner Publishing Pty. Ltd.
Burra Creek, NSW, Australia
1993

Turpin-Delport, Lesley
Satin and Silk Ribbon Embroidery
Triple T Publishing
Cape Town, South Africa
1993

INSPIRATIONAL

Embroidered Motifs

The books listed below offer a wealth of information for motifs to embroider onto crazy-quilt patches. I have referred to these books often over the years for inspiration, ideas and adaptations for embroidered patches. I highly recommend these titles to include in a personal library.

Beck, Thomasina
The Embroiderer's Flowers
David & Charles plc
Newton Abbot, Devon, England
1992

Beck, Thomasina
The Embroiderer's Garden
David & Charles plc
Newton Abbot, Devon, England
1988

Benn, Elizabeth
Treasures from the Embroiderer's Guild Collection
Charles & David plc
Newton Abbot, Devon, England
1991

Christopher, Barbara
Traditional Chinese Designs
Dover Publications, Inc.
New York, New York
1987

D'Addetta, Joseph
Traditional Japanese Design Motifs
Dover Publications, Inc.
New York, New York
1984

Gualt, Carol
Needlework Dragons and other Mythical Creatures
Van Nostrand Reinhold Company, Inc.
New York, New York
1983

Lampe, Diana
with Fisk, Jane
Embroidered Garden Flowers
Sally Milner Publishing Pty. Ltd.
Burra Creek, NSW, Australia
1991

Lampe, Diana
More Embroidered Garden Flowers
formerly *Embroider a Garden*
Sally Milner Publishing Pty. Ltd.
Burra Creek, NSW, Australia
1993

McMorris, Penny
Crazy Quilts
Dutton Studio Press

New York, New York
1984

Nichols, Marion
Designs and Patterns for Embroiderers and Craftsmen
Dover Publications, Inc.
New York, New York
1974

Phillips, Barty
Fabrics and Wallpapers, Sources, Design and Inspirations
Random Century Group
London, England
1991

Stevens, Helen M.
The Embroiderer's Countryside
David & Charles plc
Newton Abbot, Devon, England
1992

Stevens, Helen M.
The Embroiderer's Country Album
David & Charles plc
Newton Abbot, Devon, England
1994

Cross Stitch

Afghan Safari I
Afghan Safari II
Graphworks International, Inc.
Goodlettsville, Tennessee

The Roosevelt Bear books

Eaton, Seymour
Illustrated by V. Floyd Campbell
The Roosevelt Bears: Their Travels and Adventures
Edward Stern & Company, Inc.
Philadelphia, Pennsylvania
1906
reprinted by
Dover Publications, Inc.
New York, New York
1979

Eaton, Seymour
Illustrated by R.K. Culver
More about Teddy B. and Teddy G. The Roosevelt Bears Being Volume Two, Depicting their further Travels and Adventures
Edward Stern & Company, Inc.
Philadelphia, Pennsylvania
1907
reprinted under the title
The Roosevelt Bears Go to Washington
Dover Publications, Inc.
New York, New York
1981

The Movie Crazy Quilt embroidered patches were inspired by:

Barrick, Helan
Little Whippersnappers
Homespun Patterns
Chagrin Falls, Ohio
1983

Beck, Thomasina
The Embroiderer's Garden
David & Charles plc
Newton Abbot, Devon, England
1988

Bradford, Jenny
Textured Embroidery
Sally Milner Publishing Pty. Ltd.
Burra Creek, NSW, Australia
1993

Lampe, Diana
More Embroidered Garden Flowers
formerly *Embroider a Garden*
Sally Milner Publishing Pty. Ltd.
Burra Creek, NSW, Australia
1993

Montano, Judith
The Crazy Quilt Handbook
C&T Publishing
Lafayette, California
1986

Nichols, Marion
Designs and Patterns for Embroiderers and Craftsmen
Dover Publications, Inc.
New York, New York
1974

Stevens, Helen M.
The Embroiderer's Countryside
David & Charles plc
Newton Abbot, Devon, England
1992

Where Love Resides
Wedding Quilt Pattern

The pattern for the Marriage block from the Where Love Resides wedding quilt was originally designed by Barbara Brown as one of the fifteen blocks for The Life Before story quilt. This pattern is available from:

The Quilt Connection
P. O. Box 465
Odenton, Maryland 21113
410-674-8226

The remaining Where Love Resides pattern may be found in:
Pieces of an American Quilt
C & T Publishing
Lafayette, California
1996

Magazines

Inspirations—The World's Most Beautiful Embroidery
Country Bumpkin Publications
Rose Park, South Australia
Phone: 08-8364-1075
E-mail: cbumpkin@ozemail.com.au

PieceWork
Interweave Press
Loveland, Colorado
Phone: 1-800-645-3675
Website: www.interweave.com

Quilter's Newsletter Magazine
Leman Publications, Inc.
Golden, Colorado
Phone: 1-800-477-6089 or 303-604-1464
Website: www.quiltersnewsletter.com

RESEARCH RESOURCES

Brackman, Barbara
Clues In the Calico: A Guide to Identifying and Dating Antique Quilts
EPM Publications, Inc.
McLean, Virginia
1989

North Carolina Quilts
Edited by Ruth Haislip Roberson
University of North Carolina Press
Chapel Hill, North Carolina
1988

Steger, Samuel
Caldwell County, Kentucky
Turner Publishing Company
Paducah, Kentucky
1987

National Archives and Records
Administration
Pacific Region (Laguna Niguel)
24000 Avila Road
Laguna Niguel, California 92677-3497
Phone: 949-360-2641

Quote from the novel:
Otto, Whitney
How to Make an American Quilt
Random House, Inc.
New York, New York
1991

ASSOCIATIONS

American Quilt Study Group
35th and Holdrege, East Campus Loop
P.O. Box 4737
Lincoln, Nebraska 68504-0737
Phone: 402-472-5361
E-mail: AQSG@juno.com

Crazy Quilt Society
P.O. Box 19452
Omaha, Nebraska 68119
Phone: 1-800-599-0094 or 402-551-0386
Fax: 1-800-811-1610 or 402-551-0971
E-mail: QuiltHF@aol.com
Website: www.crazyquilt.com

The Embroiderers' Guild of America, Inc.
335 West Broadway, Suite 100
Louisville, Kentucky 40202
Phone: 502-589-6956
Fax: 502-584-7900
E-mail: EGAHQ@aol.com

The International Quilt Association
7660 Woodway, Suite 550
Houston, Texas 77063
Phone: 713-781-6882
Fax: 713-781-8182
E-mail: iqa@quilts.com